GLOBAL COMPANIES

 The American Assembly, *Columbia University*

GLOBAL
COMPANIES
THE POLITICAL ECONOMY
OF WORLD BUSINESS

Prentice-Hall, Inc., *Englewood Cliffs, New Jersey*

A SPECTRUM BOOK

Library of Congress Cataloging in Publication Data
MAIN ENTRY UNDER TITLE:

Global companies.

  (A Spectrum Book)
  Papers prepared for the 47th American Assembly, held
at Arden House, Columbia University, Dec., 1974.
  Includes bibliographical references and index.
  1. International business enterprises—Addresses,
essays, lectures.   2. Business and politics—Addresses,
essays, lectures.   I. American Assembly.
HD69.I7G55   338.8′8   75-5557
ISBN 0-13-357145-9
ISBN 0-13-357137-8 pbk.

10   9   8   7   6   5   4   3   2   1

PRENTICE-HALL INTERNATIONAL, INC. *(London)*
PRENTICE-HALL OF AUSTRALIA PTY., LTD. *(Sydney)*
PRENTICE-HALL OF CANADA, LTD. *(Toronto)*
PRENTICE-HALL OF INDIA PRIVATE LIMITED *(New Delhi)*
PRENTICE-HALL OF JAPAN, INC. *(Tokyo)*
PRENTICE-HALL OF SOUTHEAST ASIA (PTE.), LTD. *(Singapore)*

Table of Contents

Preface

The global company—also called the multinational corporation (MNC), the extranational enterprise (ENE), the transnational company, cosmocorp, and other names good and bad—is by no means a new phenomenon. The export of goods and services is an age-old practice. Before the twentieth century, companies in manufacturing, extractive, and service industries were to some extent operating abroad. It is the current wide reach of the practice that has called so much attention to it. Facilitated by astonishing technological advances, new management methods, better transport, and rapid communication, international business in all its phases has surged to a new high since World War II. And now hundreds of companies—chiefly American, European, and Japanese —operate all over the world.

These companies are not all alike; they take many forms. But although attitudes toward them may vary a great deal, from the political to the economic, these attitudes tend to assume that there *is* such a thing as *the* multinational corporation and to evaluate it as such. To one observer, it is "the most highly efficient mechanism for allocating and using world resources." To another observer, efforts to organize for peace are hopeless in a world of nationalism, and if we are ever going to have an international order, it will have to rest on a new extranational body—the corporation whose "manager, governors, and authorities think in extranational terms, whose personnel are indifferent to the nation-states except as impediments." Another observer sees the global company as a contributor to economic recession. Another thinks it politically stronger than the host state in which it operates, and a government unto itself. Another asserts it has no political influence at all and needs the backing of its home government. And so on.

In any event, despite a great deal of attention and a great deal of heat, not as much light has been generated as there can and should be. Not enough people know enough facts about global companies, and those who do sometimes reach opposite conclusions on the basis of the same facts. Opinion is often bemused. And so we asked George W. Ball, former Under

Secretary of State, to put this book together to help clarify some of the tough issues involving the multinationals. These papers were originally prepared for the participants in the Forty-seventh American Assembly, which met at Arden House in December 1974. (Their report of policy recommendations can be had by writing us.) It is now offered to a wider public in the hope that it will add some reliable information to the national dialogue.

The volume is not a tightly organized and integrated study but a symposium by competent authorities, each free to express himself independently. There is no unity of view. Nonetheless there is significant unity in broad premises, as we think Mr. Ball makes clear in his editing and in his transitional paragraphs between chapters.

The American Assembly has no answers of its own on the problems of the multinational corporation or indeed on any matter which it presents for public discussion, nor is it an agency of propaganda. The Assembly is a national public affairs forum that exists to provide information and encourage free exchange of ideas. We trust this book will help foster that process.

> Clifford C. Nelson
> *President*
> The American Assembly

George W. Ball

Introduction

The inarticulate premise that justifies the multinational corporation is that the political boundaries of nation-states are too narrow and constrictive to provide adequate scope for modern, large-scale economic activities. In a thoroughly pragmatic spirit businessmen have improvised the institution they need to shake free from strangling political impediments. To serve the global activities of modern business they have exploited and extended the fiction of the corporation—that artificial person which lawyers invented so that entrepreneurs could do business with limited liability and could thus mobilize capital from diverse financial sources.

Originally the corporation was conceived as a privilege granted by the state to serve its own political purposes, but over the years the widespread acceptance of the institution has enabled giant corporations to roam the world with substantial freedom, producing and selling their goods in a multiplicity of national markets, and begetting corporate offspring of various nationalities in unlimited numbers.

Today we are just beginning to realize the potential of this emancipated corporate person. For more than half a century a handful of great companies have bought, produced, and sold goods

GEORGE W. BALL, partner of Lehman Brothers, was Undersecretary of State, 1961–1966. Since being admitted to the Bar in 1934, Mr. Ball has engaged in the private practice of law or served various U.S. governmental agencies. In 1968 he was U.S. Permanent Representative to the United Nations. That year he published The Discipline of Power. Another book on foreign affairs, in addition to the one at hand, will be off the press next spring.

around the world. But since the Second World War, their number has multiplied manyfold. Today a large and rapidly expanding roster of companies is engaged in transforming the raw materials produced in one group of countries with the labor and plant facilities in others to manufacture goods it can sell in third country markets—and, with the benefit of instant communications, quick transport, computers, and modern managerial techniques, is reshuffling resources and altering the pattern on almost a month-to-month basis in response to shifting costs, prices, and availabilities.

At a time when the demand for goods of every kind is multiplying almost at a geometric rate while world resources remain finite, it is essential that we find the means to use those resources with a maximum efficiency and a minimum of waste or face a Malthusian debacle on a global scale. It is here that the multinational corporation provides mankind with a valuable instrument. Yet today it is under attack from several quarters. Some challenge its efficiency; others believe that efficiency which leads merely to the greater production of goods and services is not enough—that there are higher purposes, such as the more equitable distribution of income and other social goals, which the multinational corporation does not effectively advance.

But the most important opposition comes from those who see it as a rival to the nation-state whose authority it overlaps. It is essential that we devise the means—through new practices, new rules of conduct, or new institutions—to reconcile this conflict. In other words we must search out the ways by which we can best preserve and advance the value of the multinational corporation within the present and prospective world political structure without excessive loss to other values in which men place considerable store.

That is the objective of this book: to consider the multinational corporation not merely as a convenient industrial or commercial device but as an instrument that men can use in harmony with their political institutions to help meet the urgent requirements of a world of limited abundance where men must efficiently use the resources provided by nature if civilization is to survive. At the same time an attempt will be made to determine where the multinational company fits in the prevailing concept of world order and what new mechanisms, if any, may be needed to give legitimacy to its actions and decisions.

Eugene V. Rostow and George W. Ball

1

The Genesis
of the Multinational Corporation

E. V. R.: Evolution of the Concept

The term *multinational company* is a curious misnomer. Like many other linguistic anomalies, however, it has become part of all modern languages.

Typically, the modern multinational company is incorporated in one of the nations of Europe, one of the states of the United States, or in Japan, Taiwan, Hong Kong, or Canada. Panama, Liberia, and Nassau are the legal domicile for a number of such companies, especially in shipping and insurance. In legal personality, therefore, the multinational company is not multinational at all. Its authority derives from the law of a single state, coupled with rights granted to it by the host nations in which it is permitted to carry on business.

The history of the joint stock company is a fascinating illustration of the way in which law responds to changing social needs. Corporations are of course ancient devices—aggregations of people and property treated by the law as entities somehow distinct from

EUGENE V. ROSTOW *is Sterling Professor of Law and Public Affairs at Yale University and president of the Atlantic Treaty Association. In 1966–1969 he was Undersecretary of State for Political Affairs. Dr. Rostow has written six books and numerous articles on law and international affairs.*

the individuals who direct them. With rare exceptions, mainly for fraud or undercapitalization, liability for debts or wrongs is limited to the property publicly declared to be that of the corporation. The activities of the corporation are confined, more or less effectively, to the powers granted to it by the state. And the legal philosophers never tire of arguing about whether a corporation is a "person" for various purposes of the law.

At earlier stages in the evolution of modern capitalism, the most important corporations were either ecclesiastical, educational, or international in reach. In the eyes of the law, the property of the Church in each of its administrative areas was deemed to be vested in the person of the responsible Bishop, as a "corporation sole." Colleges and universities were similarly established as perpetual corporate bodies pursuant to statute or decree, and governed by designated groups of men, who were not liable for the debts or wrongs of the corporate body save in exceptional circumstances.

The true ancestors of the modern multinational companies, however, are not the churches, colleges and universities, guilds, or other Roman, medieval, or post-medieval examples of the capacity of the law to create "artificial persons," but the great trading companies of the seventeenth and eighteenth centuries—the East India Company, the Hudson Bay Company, La Compagnie des Indes, The Company of Adventurers of London Trading into Africa, and their Spanish, Russian, Italian, and German analogues. Many of these companies undertook to govern as well as to trade. In modern times, however, they have been exclusively economic in their activities.

With the progress of the industrial revolution and the immense shift from agriculture to industry in Europe and America, men began to perceive the need for a more effective way to form corporations than by a special legislative charter. Corporations had long been familiar to the law for special circumstances. As the nineteenth century progressed, railway companies and canal companies were established by the same procedures which had been used earlier to charter Oxford and Cambridge colleges and the great trading companies which played so large a part in the process of imperial expansion. But the industrial revolution required the flexibility of the corporation on a totally new scale. Doing business as an individual proprietor or a partnership was practical enough in predominantly agricultural societies which were engaged in relatively little commerce, and less manufacturing. A new legal framework, based on the concept of limited liability, was needed to facilitate the development of the risky modern technological economy spawned by the industrial revolution.

The super-obvious is always the most difficult of conditions to perceive. A nameless hero of American legal history produced the super-obvious answer to the economic need of the time. In 1811, he persuaded the legislature of New York to pass a statute authorizing the creation of corporations not by the enactment of special legislation, but by the simple process of filing simple documents of incorporation with a state official. State permission to establish corporations ceased to be a matter of high politics, and sometimes of corruption, and became a routine affair of bureaucracy. By 1850, the New York practice was common throughout the United States; in the same period, comparable methods for establishing corporations by a filing procedure under general statutes were accepted in the law of Great Britain, France, Germany, and other countries.

G. W. B.: The Constitutional Development of the American Common Market

Easy procedures for the creation of corporations would not by themselves have led to the great American companies of today had not the Founding Fathers—without being fully aware of what they were doing—established the conditions that made possible the modern American economy by writing two key provisions into the Constitution. One prohibited the states from laying duties or imposts on imports or exports; the other delegated to the Congress the power to regulate interstate commerce—a power which the Supreme Court by a series of decisions over many years was to elaborate and expand to meet the needs of a developing continent.

Reinforcing one another, these provisions assumed that the market in which business could flourish would be defined by the broad boundaries of the nation rather than the constricting borders of individual states. To acclaim this as one of the major decisions of that critical year in Philadelphia involves some sterile speculative assumptions. Yet—absent action of some other kind—it seems possible that, had the Constitution not contained these provisions, the United States would, in economic terms, have become little more than a kind of Germanic Federation without even a dominant Prussia to impose a *Zollverein*.

Because the individual American states were smaller in population than many of the nations of Western Europe, the nation's economy might well have suffered from arrested development. It would have been clearly impossible to build efficient industries exploiting the economies of scale within markets defined by constrictive state lines. Moreover, since economic and political fragmentation go hand in hand, one can even speculate that, if the individual states had been permitted to establish their own protected markets, the political glue that held them together might have proved inadequate.

In a very real sense, the Constitution came in the nick of time; because even by 1789 the new states were developing mercantilist habits. A farmer carting cordwood from Connecticut to New York was stopped at the state line and made to pay duty. Another farmer barging a load of pigs across the Hudson from New York had to pay a tariff when his cargo reached the Jersey shore.

It was another example of where the young lawyer-politicians convened in Philadelphia reacted to a prophetic instinct. By forbidding the states to interfere with the nationwide growth of enterprise, they prepared America for the explosive expansion that accompanied the wide use of machinery. Once the Civil War had fractured old patterns, free-wheeling entrepreneurs struck out with energy and confidence to supply the burgeoning needs of an expanding nation, and, by the end of the nineteenth century, America was quite prepared to challenge the older industry of Europe on its own territory. Indeed we find a British writer as early as 1901 already bewailing the "American invasion." "The most serious aspect of the American industrial invasion," wrote Mr. Fred A. McKenzie, "lies in the fact that these newcomers have acquired control of every new industry created during the past fifteen years. In old trades we are hard put to it to hold our own; in the new we are scarcely making any pretense at doing so."

European industrialists had no great free market in which to expand; unlike America, the nation-states that emerged in Western Europe were not organized on a continent-wide basis. To be sure, enterprises sold their wares across national boundaries but largely in the traditional form of exports, while only a few European companies had the vigor and foresight to establish sources of production outside their home country.

It was inevitable, therefore, that American firms, with a wide continent in which to operate and maneuver, should have learned concepts of scale and magnitude far exceeding those common in European business. Meanwhile a few American companies—particularly in the new and more dynamic sectors—had the audacity to build plants and facilities overseas. For the others the American market provided all the challenge and opportunity required.

This abruptly changed with the Second World War. Then many Americans gained familiarity with Europe through our military involvement, while at home there was, in certain sectors, a vast expansion of production to meet wartime needs. Emerging from the war with an intact industrial plant and a new sense of scope and scale, American businessmen developed not only a wider interest in overseas market but a greater self-confidence in expanding operations beyond the confines of their home country.

No doubt the impulse to expand around the world was also greatly stimulated by our new feeling of world mission—awareness that America was the world's most powerful nation and that we had vast responsibilities in almost every corner of the globe. And, finally, to all this was added computers and the other tools of increasingly sophisticated management that made it possible to control and direct operation thousands of miles from home base.

It was therefore no accident that American entrepreneurs should begin to think in global terms—not merely in terms of national markets but of the world market. No longer was it a question of producing at home and exporting overseas; new possibilities emerged for deploying the factors of production on a global scale—the opportunity to find and use materials, machines, capital, and management with a new flexibility that took little account of the limits imposed by the political boundaries of nation-states which were much too confining for modern enterprise.

But just as it was inevitable that great enterprises should feel driven to organize themselves on a world scale, it was also inevitable that there would be an increasing collision between multinational corporations and nation-states. Even though created by private initiative and with no political objectives of their own, corporations that buy, sell, and produce abroad do have the power to affect the lives of peoples and of nations in a manner that necessarily challenges the prerogatives and responsibilities of political authority.

Quite likely, had national governments continued, as in the *laissez-faire* atmosphere of the nineteenth century, to confine their interests and activities to the advancement of empire and the protection of the lives and properties of the citizenry, this collision of competing sovereignties would have resulted in only minimal trouble. But, simultaneously with the rapid flowering of the multinational corporation, has come a vast extension and expansion of the responsibilities and activities of governments. Obviously, the degree to which governments interfere in the market place varies widely, depending on the traditions and political complexion of the particular country, but a high degree of interference is now almost universal.

Inevitably these two developments—the broadening of governmental responsibility and the rapid expansion of the multinational company—have resulted in a competition and, ultimately, a collision of sovereignties. How can a national government be expected to sit calmly by while a corporate management—based 5,000 miles away—is able, by its decisions, to affect the prosperity of the country over which that government presides? Who can expect local political authority, in other words, to permit absentee managements to interfere with national economic plans, create or diminish employment, and, by their decisions, materially affect the foreign exchange earnings and, hence, the balance of payments of the country in question?

These questions have, of course, more relevance for small countries than for large ones, since, if the economy is both substantial and diversified, individual enterprise is unlikely to have a major impact on national policy as a whole; yet in countries medium-sized now but large by nineteenth century standards the effect on individual industrial sectors may still be substantial, and when the industries concerned are particularly sensitive because of considerations of national defense or even national pride, some reaction from the government in question may be expected.

These questions go to the legitimacy of the power of absentee corporate management—indeed, to the legitimacy of the power of multinational corporations. In the course of this book an attempt will be made to consider these questions in more detail, but first it may be useful to examine the *raison d'être* of the multinational corporation as it appears to its own managers.

Jacques G. Maisonrouge

2

How a Multinational Corporation
Appears to Its Managers

If, as Edward Gibbon observed, history is "little more than the register of the crimes, follies and misfortunes of mankind," ours is surely an era that future scholars will study with zeal. For in the last few years we have witnessed the rise of a series of problems that, for range, complexity, and seriousness, have seldom been equalled.

Pandemic inflation, skyrocketing oil prices, scarcities of raw materials, disequilibrium in international payments, poor harvests, rising unemployment, high interest rates, growing fear of a global depression—these are only some of the problems currently bedeviling the human race. Nor are they confined to the developed countries. Speaking of the prospects for the poorest billion people in the world, Robert S. McNamara, president of the World Bank, recently said that they face "appalling deprivation" and "the risk of death" as food is priced out of their reach and aid programs are reduced by the industrialized nations.

While our politicians, economists, and assorted ideologues ponder

Jacques G. Maisonrouge *is chairman and chief executive officer of the IBM World Trade Europe/Middle East/Africa Corporation. Director of several other business corporations, he is also an executive vice president of the French Chamber of Commerce in the United States. Mr. Maisonrouge is a trustee of the Institute of International Education and an officer of the International Management Education Foundation.*

these dilemmas and seek solutions, they appear only to grow worse. Indeed, if current trends are extrapolated to the year 2000 and beyond, the prospects are, at best, discouraging.

The seminal problem appears to be the lopsided distribution of the world's resources, both material and human. What is needed are mechanisms whereby those resources can be identified, managed, and more equitably distributed.

One such mechanism—the international company—already exists, but ironically it is being increasingly viewed by governments and supranational agencies alike as part of the problem. Thus, it has been variously characterized as a manipulator of currencies, an exporter of jobs and technologies, a secret instrument of home country policies, exploiter of developing economies, a dodger of taxes, and a creator of artificial shortages.

Some of us, however, perceive the international company in a quite different light, as a prophetic forerunner of a better world, and I should like to consider the company in some detail as the engine primarily responsible for powering our global economy.

It may not be especially insightful to observe that the destinies of nations have become inextricably tied to each other. The recent monetary, energy, and food crises have only been the latest demonstrations of that fact. And if it is still useful to remember that the world we live in is growing smaller all the time, it may also be to the point to recall that astronomers have characterized Earth as a fifth-rate planet revolving around a third-rate star in a second-rate solar system tucked away in a remote corner of the universe.

But it is the only world we have and to manage this speck of cosmic dust in such a way that its inhabitants can live decently, with dignity and in peace, each with his fair share of what the world has to offer, is extremely challenging work, worthy of our best efforts. It is my contention that no better tool has yet been devised for realizing these goals than the international company. I say this for two reasons.

First, given human nature, the international company harnesses several of our deepest instincts—self interest, competitiveness, the need to be part of something bigger than ourselves—on behalf of the greatest good.

Second, in view of the sorry record of generations of politicians trying to solve the same problems—hunger, disease, illiteracy, the unequal distribution of wealth—it is all too clear that purely political solutions do not work in the long run. Certainly, the energy crisis has demonstrated beyond dispute that in time of internal difficulties, most governments promptly place national interests, or their views of them, ahead of long-term international cooperation.

Although the international company is by no means new, it is only in the last 10 or 15 years that it has really come of age in the sense of operating within a concept of global planning. Furthermore, it is a logical response to some of the more important facts of contemporary life.

On the economic level, there has been a growing need to rely on larger markets to offset research and development costs. The British aircraft industry, for instance, cannot survive if it cannot sell abroad. For most countries, the same holds true in shipbuilding, automobile manufacture, and the computer industry.

On the political level, internationalism is a trend of our times. We see it in the formation of such organizations as the EEC, OECD, and ANCOM. We even see it in the slowly growing détente between the United States and Russia, which are beginning to trade and join in cooperative ventures in space and ecological research. Admittedly, there are clear and present threats of a protectionist revival today, but historically speaking, since the end of World War II, the broad trend has been toward freer trade.

On the technological level, common information made instantly available to the peoples of the developed countries has cut across national boundaries and generated the same economic appetites, aspirations, and demands. Even in the less developed countries, we find a persistent demand today for the very latest technologies. At the same time, such achievements as the jet airplane, satellite communications, and computers have made it possible for a company to control far-flung enterprises.

Finally, *on the social level*, thanks to better communications, swifter travel, and more education, people—particularly young people—are shedding the parochialism of their fathers. Despite the crosswinds of nationalism, regionalism, and blocism, there is a growing understanding that ours is really one indivisible world.

In many ways, the international company has been in the vanguard of this movement toward internationalism. In the process, it is helping to build a new world economic system, one in which the constraints of geography are giving way, sometimes reluctantly, to the logic of efficiency.

In the popular mind, "international company" has become virtually synonymous with "American"—a fallacious identification given wide currency some years ago by Mr. Servan-Schreiber's book, *The American Challenge.* What he failed to realize at the time was that the growth of the American business role in Europe was just the visible tip of a broader trend. Manufacturing companies from many countries were moving factors of production, not just goods, into the markets of other countries. European, Japanese, and Canadian, as well as American international activity, was globalizing production in all parts of the world. By the end of 1973, for example, European direct investments in the United States alone had a book value of $12.16 billion.

As a result of this trend, new flows of capital and goods, parts and components are circulating in ever more complex patterns among subsidiaries and branches of corporations that straddle the earth. Typical of the new pattern is Canada's Massey-Ferguson, which manufactures tractors in the United States for sale in Canada; they contain British-made engines, French transmissions, and Mexican axles.

By now, the magnitude of international business is staggering, recent estimates place the value of international output at more than $500 billion a year. Even more significant than the amount itself, however, is the fact that international operations continue to grow at twice the economic growth rates of the industrialized nations, and faster than world trade in general. The clear implication is that world production is being internationalized at a brisk pace. Projections of growth rates suggest that, within a generation, more than half of the free world's production may be internationalized. Moreover, if the dynamism of the international sector can be maintained, its growth is bound to generate an increasingly powerful stimulus on growth rates all around. And despite the increasing suspicion and criticism that the "cult" of growth has been subjected to recently, it still represents our best hope for the future, not because growth by and of itself is desirable, but because many of its by-products are. Among those by-products are the creation of new jobs, new wealth, and higher living standards, which in turn result in closing the various gaps—economic, educational, and technological—that have always fueled human jealousy, hatred, and conflicts.

International companies benefit their home countries, too. In 1973, for example, the $10 billion improvement in the United States' basic balance of payments was largely due to the $10.8 billion in royalties, fees, and investment income generated by American international firms, as well as to United States' exports by international companies in such high-technology industries as nonelectric machinery ($5.2 billion), aircraft and parts ($3.4 billion), and computers and parts ($1.5 billion). The conclusion is inescapable: America's strength in the world marketplace has been largely due to its high technology-based international companies. So, even as they themselves grow, such corporations do a great deal of good. And the most important role they play is probably that of great equalizers among nations. As a result, they serve as catalysts of progress.

Let me get more specific and describe the experiences of the international company I know best—IBM Corporation, which is considered one of the most typical of international firms. In addition to IBM's extensive operations and facilities in the United States:

—We operate in 126 countries overseas with some 125,000 employees;
—we do business in 30 languages, in more than 100 currencies;
—we have 23 plants in 13 countries;
—we have 8 development laboratories in as many countries;
—and we have a very healthy offshore growth rate, going from $51 million in gross income in 1950 to $5.14 billion in 1973. In fact, since 1970 our overseas business has accounted for more than half the corporation's net income.

Despite the company's geographical dispersion, there is scarcely any event, however remote, that does not have some impact on the total company: currency devaluations and revaluations; a variety of international tensions; natural disasters such as floods and earthquakes; strikes; military coups; civil wars; and the like. In addition, a variety of business practices, customs, and national characteristics compound the complexity of our business environment. Since their beginnings, our operations abroad have been carried out by nationals in each of the countries in which we do business. In most countries, and certainly in all the larger ones, our people are local citizens, from the president down to the last clerk.

We believe that giving these responsibilities to local nationals makes us more sensitive to the market, simplifies our dealings with governments, and improves our image. Above all, we believe it enables us to operate as responsive and responsible citizens in the countries where we do business.

At the same time, our organizational structure is designed to take advantage of the talents of our international population. Thus, our business outside the United States is conducted by two Group Corporations: IBM World Trade Europe/Middle East/Africa Corporation and IBM World Trade Americas/Far East Corporation, with their headquarters in New York. However, IBM World Trade Europe/Middle East/Africa Corporation has its principal management team in Paris. Each headquarters has an international staff. Management not only benefits from the diverse knowledge and cross-fertilization of ideas bred in such an environment, but assignees to these headquarters receive valuable training which they take back to their countries, adding to local management strength there.

IBM is unique among internationals in a number of ways. Its primary product, for example, is knowledge—not hardware. And it is essentially a service company.

Its size and position of leadership in its industry have made it highly visible. And because the computer industry is so basic a tool in the modern economy, vital to other high-technology industries, IBM Corporation is especially subject to economic nationalism.

As a result, we not only have to contend with its usual manifestations, but have encountered some special ones. Local manufacturers of data processing equipment in Germany, France, the United Kingdom, and Japan, for example, are heavily subsidized by their governments. Public procurement policies in those countries favor local manufacturers. And the EEC is promoting the development of a European computer industry that can compete with its United States counterparts and make Europe independent in this area. Nevertheless, we have been successful and have generally been given high marks by host governments and competitors alike. There are a number of reasons for this, but none is more important than our contributions toward economic and social progress.

What, precisely, do we do?

1. *We provide employment for some 125,000 people* outside the United States. In the process, we generate salaries, pay local taxes, both direct and indirect, and upgrade employee skills—facts not normally identified in national economic statistics.

2. *We serve as a vehicle for the transfer of technology,* which we develop worldwide, then inject into various national economies. As a result, we tend to raise productivity, equalize wages, working conditions, and ultimately, living standards. And by narrowing the gaps between nations, we also believe that we are contributing to peace.

We transfer technology in a number of ways—for example, through direct investment; through our development laboratories; through the training of both customers and employees in the concepts, applications, and management of computers and other information-handling equipment; and through substantial purchases from local vendors and subcontractors, whose technology we often help upgrade by setting standards, suggesting manufacturing and testing equipment, training personnel, and consulting on particular problems.

3. *We help developing countries grow.* Governments themselves are often major IBM customers. Worldwide computer industry statistics indicate that government installations account for about 9 percent of total computer sales. But in many developing countries, this figure may reach as high as 90 to 100 percent. By the very nature of the service we offer, therefore, we help developing economies cross the threshold of modernization and step into the new territory of self-sustained growth. In Indonesia, for example, computers are

being used for oil exploration; in Peru, to revive the vital fish meal industry; in Argentina, to improve medical services.

4. *Through our 11 scientific centers in 8 countries, we are cooperating with governments and academic communities* in seeking solutions to some of the world's most pressing problems. The United Kingdom Scientific Center in Peterlee, for instance, specializes in applying computer technology to such areas as environmental control and urban planning. The German Scientific Center at Heidelberg has been working with the German Cancer Research Center at the University of Heidelberg on cancer detection and diagnostics. And, in Madrid, the Spanish Scientific Center is investigating the reduction of air and noise pollution.

5. *We have made our expertise available.* While there is no longer any real "technology gap" between the advanced nations, there *is* a massive need for technology and know-how in the world's developing countries. In the area of our expertise, we have supported workshops in the computing sciences, particularly in Latin America. We bring in teachers who work with their local colleagues and we donate time, money, and computer equipment to universities to set up computer centers.

On the business level, in developing countries where full-time education facilities are not available, instruction programs are offered to customers on an "as needed" basis, with local IBM marketing representatives and systems engineers serving as instructors. Customer courses in the developing countries range from basic machine operation to sophisticated programming techniques.

6. *We have not reached our position in any world market through acquisitions or mergers.* There is considerable resentment of the high level of United States investment which has been made in various countries—a resentment, ironically, that is now also surfacing in the United States as the amount of foreign investment here grows. This resentment is accentuated when the investment takes the form of a take-over of a well-known local company as a way of establishing a position in the local market. In the case of IBM, we started our operations from scratch in each country and feel that we have, in fact, played a major role in developing the data processing market and competence in the major countries. For example, we are not

latecomers to international operations; we started in Japan and the Philippines in 1926, in Denmark in 1921, and even had a manufacturing operation in Canada in the early 1920s and in France in 1922. Our growth, in short, has been attained in the biblical manner—by "the sweat of our brow." It has been entirely due to our own efforts, our desire to grow, and the acceptance of our products and services in the marketplace.

There are many more things that we do, but these should serve to illustrate the nature of our efforts. And what is true of IBM is also true of many other international companies. In short, as a result of its activities, the international company emerges not only as an important closer of gaps, but as a force for world understanding and, therefore, peace because it contributes to the reduction of economic and military conflicts between nations. It does this in at least four important ways:

1. The movement of people from country to country that it fosters broadens their experience, outlook, and understanding of others.
2. The flow of capital around the world that it generates increases the interdependence of economies and the commonality of national interests.
3. Through the transfer of technology, as I have already indicated, it reduces the economic and social gaps between countries.
4. And the infusion of modern management techniques for which it is responsible helps close the "management gap," thereby increasing knowledge of how to maximize the use of resources.

Unfortunately, we have not yet found a solution to the problem of the developing nations. Their chronically high birth rate tends to dilute per capita GNP gains, and all forecasters seem to agree that by 1980 the gap between developing countries and the leading industrial states will be even greater than it is today. Many international companies have invested in developing countries, to be sure. IBM, for example, has plants in Argentina, Brazil, Colombia, India, and Mexico and is the largest exporter of finished goods in both Argentina and Brazil.

Nevertheless, the developing countries will remain a major part of what the Club of Rome has called the "world problematique" for many years to come. No easy answers can be anticipated. But precisely because the problem is global and so complex, the solution can only be reached on an international level, a level on which, by definition, no single nation-state—regardless of its wealth or power—can operate effectively.

But until a concerted effort *is* made on a political-economic-social level, international companies are, in many ways, showing the way. They are showing the way because, from the outset, they have viewed the world as it really is: one great system, whose human and material resources have, unfortunately, been distributed unequally. Within that environment they have learned to plan, produce, and market globally, allocating those resources irrespective of national frontiers in order to find the most effective pattern of production worldwide.

The future of the world is not foreordained. Man has the power to weigh alternatives, choose the best possible scenario, and make it happen. If we are to have a twenty-first century in which the world's inequities begin to be resolved, in which reason supplants passion, and humanity's problems are tackled on a truly global basis, then new approaches and new mechanisms must be utilized.

I submit that the modern international company is one of the best of these mechanisms and, on the basis of past performance as well as future promise, ought to be allowed to work. It is an idea whose time is fast approaching.

Ronald Müller

3

A Qualifying and Dissenting View of the Multinational Corporation

Because the multinational corporations are both conspicuous and powerful they have necessarily stirred up considerable controversy. Where Mr. Maisonrouge sees the internationalization of business as the wave of the future, others view it with apprehension. Balancing the appraisal is the following chapter by Professor Ronald E. Müller, who holds the emergence of global companies accountable for much of the failure of United States fiscal and economic policy.

G. W. B.

Recently, a growing number of writers, commissions of international agencies, and national governments have come to the conclusion that new institutional regulatory measures for the control of global corporations are necessary. An analysis of these conclusions shows that they treat separately such problem categories as transfer pricing effects on national tax revenues, interaffiliate loans and international transfers of parents' liquid assets as separate

---

RONALD MÜLLER *is professor of economics at American University. A consultant to private business firms and agencies of the U.S. government, Dr. Müller is author of* The Global Corporation and Latin American Development *(May 1975) and co-author with R. J. Barnet of* Global Reach: The Power of the Multinational Corporations.

and not necessarily interrelated components of regulation. With few exceptions, the question has yet to be asked whether such problems are but manifestations of a more profound *systemic* impact of the new operating characteristics of global enterprises. That is, whether the global interdependence of individual economies resulting from the globalization of their largest private corporations does not have a direct bearing on the growing inefficacy of national macroeconomic stabilization policy to maintain full employment, price stability, and balance of payment equilibrium.

This chapter addresses itself to this question from a U.S. perspective via a review of the literature on global corporations. This review derives a number of testable propositions. Taken together these propositions lead to the conclusion that since the mid-1960s macroeconomic monetary and fiscal policy for regulating the U.S. economy has had increasingly ineffective and at times perverse results. A direct causal connection is seen to hold between this policy inefficacy and the emergence of global corporations as the dominant actors of the U.S. political economy.

A major contention of this chapter is that the globalization of the world's largest private enterprises, industrial and financial alike, represents a structural transformation in the location of their activities and the manner in which they behave as institutions. In turn this structural transformation has now increased significantly the invalidity of the behavioral assumptions in the orthodox microeconomic theory of the firm, the underlying basis for modern Keynesian macroeconomic theory and therefore policy. Because these corporations account for the dominant share of economic transactions within and between nation-states, it is hypothesized that their own transformation has brought about a structural transformation of the national and international economy. This change in the behavior of the U.S. economy, including its foreign sector, means that it no longer responds in the fashion predicted by the theoretical models underlying policy-making. The major part of this chapter will present a range of empirical examples for the verification of this hypothesis. First, however, we turn to the meaning of structural transformation as it relates to our knowledge about how an economy changes its behavior over time.

Structural Change and the Nature of Transformation

This is not the first time that the U.S. political economy has undergone a structural transformation. With the development of a nationwide communications infrastructure after the Civil War, the U.S. went from a set of regionally based economies to that of a nationally integrated economy. This transformation was led by that of the local-regional firm into the large nationwide corporation. Other institutions, however, lagged behind in this transformation process. The institution of nationwide labor units lagged in their evolution, not receiving final legal recognition until after the beginning of the Great Depression. Public sector regulatory institutions were also slow in responding to the transformation underway in the private corporate sector. Commencing only in the very late 1800s, notably in the field of antitrust after the post–Civil War surge in industrial and financial concentration, there was a significant change in the regulatory functions of government over private business. Yet it was only during the depths of the Great Depression that the public sector completed its own transformation into performing the regulatory and macro-management functions of the national economy as they are known today. This "structural lag" in public sector institutions also mirrored a lag in economic theory. Again, not until the depression was well underway did economic theory experience its own transformation in the form of the Keynesian "synthesis." This was the last transformation of the U.S. political economy until that of the post-World War II period.

The Present Transformation

The present structural transformation can be identified by two sets of empirical indicators representing the *interrelated* forces of change at work. The first, taking place via its largest bank and industrial enterprises, is the globalization of the economy. Stated otherwise, the U.S. economy has undergone an historic increase in its foreign dependency. The second is the historic upsurge in the industrial and financial concentration of the domestic private sector.

The true extent of the U.S. economy's dependence on foreign operations cannot be gleaned by focusing on exports and imports as a percentage of GNP. Note rather that in 1960, the proportion of *total* corporate U.S. profits derived overseas was only 7 percent, with exponential increases commencing around 1967. Today, an estimated 30 percent of total U.S. corporate profits are derived from overseas.

Another indicator of the new global dependence of the U.S. economy is the amount of total U.S. corporate investment which goes overseas versus that at home. In 1957, foreign investment in new plant and equipment was 9 percent of *total* U.S. corporate domestic plant and equipment expenditures. By 1970, it had reached a figure of some 25 percent; again, exponential increases occur starting in the years 1965–1967. In 1961, the sales of all U.S. manufacturing abroad represented only 7 percent of total U.S. sales; by 1965, the figure had crept up to 8.5 percent; but by 1970, foreign sales were more than 13 percent of total sales of *all* U.S. manufacturing corporations. For the U.S. banking sector, current foreign dollar deposits of the nation's largest global banks are estimated at more than 65 percent of their domestic deposit holdings, up from 8.5 percent in 1960.

With a time-lag, the corporate globalization process has led to an acceleration in the rate of increase in industrial and financial concentration of the U.S. *domestic* sector. Between 1955 and 1970 the *Fortune* top 500 industrial corporations increased their share of total manufacturing and mining employment, profits, and assets from slightly more than 40 percent to over 70 percent. Whereas during the fifties the largest two hundred were increasing their share of total industrial assets each year by an average of 1 percent, by the 1960s, this annual rate of increased concentration had doubled. For 1947–1966, the largest fifty U.S. corporations increased their share of total value-added in manufacturing from 17 percent to 25 percent; the largest two hundred, from 30 to 42 percent. The momentum of cumulative concentration is in part reflected by the corporate merger movement. Of the 14,000 individual mergers during 1953–1968, the top 100 firms accounted for only 333, but acquired 35 percent of all merged assets. In the mid-1960s the merger movement accelerated at an exponential rate; almost 60 percent of the $66 billion of total merged assets between 1953–1968 were acquired in the last four years of that period. In 1965, for example, the 1,496 mergers were the highest annual increase in the history of the United States. Increases in banking concentration started somewhat later than in the industrial sector, but by 1970 the top 50 of a total of some 13,000 banks had over 48 percent of all bank assets. From 1965 to 1970 the top fifty were increasing their share of total assets at more than double their expansion rate during the previous ten years. Federal Reserve Board studies show that almost all foreign deposits of U.S. banks are in the hands of the top twenty American global banks, with four holding 38 percent of these deposits, and twelve having 83 percent of all foreign banking assets. On the lending side, the 220 largest banks account for virtually all of industrial bank loans. Nine of the largest global banks account, for example, for more than 26 percent of all total commercial and industrial lending by American banks. In addition, these same nine hold 90 percent of the entire indebtedness in the U.S. petroleum and natural gas industry, 66 percent in machinery and metal products, and 75 percent in the chemical and rubber industries.

These indicators are presented as evidence of the structural transformation of the economy itself. Globalization and concentration are not, however, the only indicators of transformation. Others, to be discussed shortly, include money flows and the use of credit. Of significance here is that an analysis of these various indicators shows that they broke their historical trend-paths sometime during the mid-1960s. This suggests that the turning point in the structural transformation of the economy occurred somewhere between 1965 and 1967; which of course correlates well with the beginning of the "stagflation" phenomenon, an occurrence unaccounted for by economic theory and thus far defying governmental policy-making corrections.

Global Corporations and the Nature of Global Corporate Competition: Policy Implications

To understand the transformed behavior of the economy, in contrast to the assumptions about its behavior embedded in policy-making, it is necessary to review the institutional characteristics of actual corporate behavior. As already noted, this is because global corporations account for the majority of the economy's transactions. If in the aggregate we understand the dynamics of the corporate sector of the economy then we have gone a long way toward understanding the behavior of the national economy and the problems of current policy. We shall proceed by focusing on the transformed goals and the actual operational means (corporate operating techniques) by which global enterprises accomplish these goals. This analysis, however, is only illuminating if done in the context of the global competitive forces that to a certain extent both constrain and determine the individual enterprise's behavior. Finally, our review of global corporate institutional characteristics can explain other aspects of the structural transformation of the national economy not yet discussed.

GLOBAL MAXIMIZATION AND NATIONAL WELFARE

When a national corporation evolves into a global one, the basic change in goals is that of maximizing the long-run profits of the parent's total global system. There is now abundant empirical evidence to demonstrate that global system profit maximization does not necessarily mean the maximization of each subsidiary's profits, at least in the sense of profits as recorded by national statistics. Thus, for example, transfer pricing permits cost minimization for the global system by shifting profits earned, but not reported, in one nation to another nation with a lower tax rate. The outcome is global tax minimization, one of the key requisites for global profit maximization. A second outcome is the negation of the classical and neoclassical theoretical proof (which underlies much of current policy), to wit: that a national production unit will be operated to maximize profits earned, declared, and accruing to the nation-state within which it is located. At the very least, therefore, the operational techniques of managing the multinational economic system of a global corporation make uncertain whether a parent's operation of any given subsidiary will be in harmony with a given country's national welfare. This uncertainty can be attached to the national welfare implications of both host and home nations alike, since the emphasis is on global system profit maximization which need not be the same as home country profit maximization.

NATIONAL POLICY: CONCENTRATION AND GLOBALIZATION

Two major and empirically well-established characteristics of global corporations are that (a) most of them are conglomerates, and (b) in the many different product groups or industries in which they operate, they compete as oligopolies, not as perfectly competitive firms. In turn oligopoly competition, as orthodox economics correctly teaches, is characterized not only by nonprice forms of competitive behavior, but more importantly for our present purposes, by a particular short-run management goal for assessing the stability of the corporations' long-term profit stream. This short-run goal of the oligopoly is minimally the maintenance or preferably the increase in its market shares vis-à-vis its other competitors. When an oligopoly, competing to maintain or increase its market share in one industry, is in fact a subsidiary of a parent conglomerate operating in many industries, the parent can choose to "cross-subsidize" the subsidiary with one or more of its three basic resources: technology (including mechanical, managerial, and accounting), finance capital, and marketing resources.

If the subsidiary is competing with other oligopoly firms that are not subsidiaries of conglomerates, then the likely systemic outcome[1] is that these nonconglomerate firms will eventually experience a decline in their market shares, go out of business or be absorbed by

---

[1] By "systemic outcome" is meant the inherent result from the interaction of various institutions with each other within the context of a given socio-economic system. Systemic here is being used in the same sense as in the works of the classical economists such as Adam Smith and Joseph Schumpeter.

conglomerate enterprises. This is true because compared to the single industry firm, the conglomerate's sheer size allows it to generate internal economies of scale which over time give it an inherent competitive advantage over smaller concerns. Such internal economies include, for example, easier and usually cheaper sources of external finance, lower effective corporate tax rates, lower input costs (*e.g.*, advertising) due to quantity discounts and/or greater expertise, greater financial leverage to sustain cyclical periods of profit decline, and/or more easily sustained losses during short-run price competition at times of initial entry to new industries. If in addition the oligopoly competition just described is between the subsidiary of a global corporation, *i.e.*, a global conglomerate, and single-industry, strictly national, oligopoly, then the systemic outcome of increasing concentration is even more likely to occur.

In the 1930s orthodox economics accepted into its fold the field of industrial organization. Since that time industrial organization economists have produced a rich empirical literature to demonstrate that cross-subsidization between subsidiaries of conglomerates is a basic practice of modern corporate life. It is also well known that wherever global corporations expand, there is usually associated with that expansion an increase in concentration. Increasing concentration takes place first in both the more and less developed host countries into which global companies expand and to which they can cross-subsidize their initial foreign entries with the resources of the parent's home network. Later, it feeds back to the home country. After a wave of foreign expansion, the global corporation can use the added internal economies of scale from its now increased size to supplement its competitiveness at home. That is, globalization leads, with a time lag, to increasing domestic concentration in the home nation. That this proposition on the systemic outcome of global oligopoly competition should be taken seriously is confirmed by recent empirical studies of the changing nature of industrial/financial organization and concentration in the countries of the European Community.

These studies show that the only way European firms could stop and/or regain declining market shares, lost during the fifties to U.S.

global corporations, was through a duplication of their American counterparts' expansion pattern of globalization and domestic mergers and acquisitions. Thus by the early sixties, after recovery from World War II, the European response to the "American Challenge" was to expand first globally and later through mergers and acquisitions in the home territory of the European Community. The timing of the historical concentration increases in the U.S. economy of the sixties would also appear to be explained by this proposition on the systemic outcome of global oligopoly competition. This concentration spurt occurred after the initial global expansions by U.S. corporations into Europe and the underdeveloped countries in the 1950s.

It is in this sense that we can understand why increasing global interdependence and concentration are interrelated aspects of the U.S. economy's structural transformation in the post-World War II period: interrelated and to be directly associated with the globalization of its largest corporations, mostly conglomerates, increasingly engaged in a new form of oligopoly competition, across nations and industries, with competitors who are more and more themselves conglomerates. Analytically restated, there is in short a *systemic and cumulative* process toward increasing global interdependence and concentration of the national economy.

Given this transformation, one notes some significant structural lags in governmental regulatory institutions and policies. For example, antitrust laws primarily emphasize horizontal and, secondarily, vertical integration, with a relative neglect of conglomerate mergers. (Of the some 14,000 mergers between 1953 and 1968, the government challenged 199 cases, won 90 of these, and required divesture in 48 instances.) In addition, as concentration proceeded over this period, there became apparent a set of "vicious circles" arising out of the impacts of Keynesian monetary and fiscal policy and leading to increasing policy inefficacy. A recent quantitative analysis of actual policy impacts by Professor John Blair verifies the mounting evidence of other econometric investigations. During the boom phase, stabilization policy is aimed at reducing inflation via a reduction in aggregate demand. The findings of Blair and others are revealing however: The more concentrated the industry, the greater has been the occurrence of continuing relative price increases, *i.e.,* the opposite of intended policy impacts.

The vicious circles inherent in fiscal and monetary policy are helpful in understanding these unintended impacts. For fiscal policy, congressional and university studies have shown that tax reductions to stimulate the economy are disproportionately absorbed by the largest firms. (Internal economies of scale can explain much of this result.) On the expenditure side, studies also reveal disproportionate amounts going to the largest firms. In both cases, the effect is to give large corporations a greater expansion capacity than smaller firms, thereby promoting further concentration. In the next round, the increased concentration leads to policy's increased ineffectiveness. The vicious circle is complete. A similar phenomenon takes place with monetary policy. On the borrowing side, during periods of credit restriction, the largest industrial firms do not (or only with a long time delay) respond to higher financing costs since their oligopoly positions permit them to pass on increased credit costs to their buyers. Smaller firms, because of their relatively weaker oligopoly power, must respond immediately and lower their investment demands. As in the case of taxes and expenditures, these differential structural impacts of aggregate policy promote further concentration. Similarly on the lending side, there are vicious circles at work. Take, for example, George Budzeika's recent findings on the behavior of the large New York City banks, published by New York University's Institute of Finance: "New York City bank behavior in the past two decades has shown that it is very difficult to control large banks whenever the demand for credit is heavy." The reasons for this again turn out to be the internal economies unique to the large but not the smaller banks which because of a "lack of information and skills prevent them from adjusting quickly to changing levels of monetary restriction." For large banks "the only way to restrain efficiently is to reduce the overall liquidity of the banking system." But since the costs in unemployment of such a strong measure are politically unacceptable, only mild monetary restraint has been pursued. This leads to further bank concentration and makes the next phase of policy restraint that much more ineffective.

MARKET POLICY IN A POST-MARKET ECONOMY

The conglomerate characteristic of global corporations and the nature of global oligopoly competition explain a third category of structural transformation. That is, that more and more of the private sector's total domestic and international transactions are between subsidiaries of the same parent corporation. Thus the global corporation is largely a *post-market enterprise,* since a significant share of its total transactions are not with independent buyers and sellers dealing at arms length through the market. Given the dominance of aggregate global corporate transactions in the domestic and foreign sector, and given the systemic outcome of increasing concentration which results from global corporate competition, it is an empirically verifiable fact that our contemporary national and world economy is becoming increasingly a *post-market economic system.*

Let us be clear what is meant by a post-market economy. It is one in which there has occurred the negation of the social *function* of the market as an institution for equilibrating the economy. Yes, there are markets in the sense of a commodity-space indicating the total number of goods produced or consumed. But in the functional sense just defined, which is the meaning of the concept as used in classical and neoclassical economics, the market has largely been negated. The function of the market as a social institution is to generate price signals through the forces of supply and demand as carried out by independent buyers and sellers. In the Keynesian synthesis, these signals are relied upon by private business people, unions, and public policy-makers as the information for guiding their decisions which govern the allocation of resources and the distribution of income. Where the market is operative, these decisions theoretically should result in full employment, price stability, and balance of payments equilibrium. *Systemically, i.e.,* neither by intent nor design, but by the outcome of modern corporate competition, global corporations are a chief source of market negation. First, by the process of increasing concentration accompanying their expansion which, as orthodox theory correctly teaches, increasingly distorts price signals. Second, intracorporate transactions negate the market's social function, by definition, because they completely bypass the market. Market negation is another significant aspect of the post-World War II structural transformation of the U.S. political economy. This transformation, however, is still incomplete for there is a notable structural lag in public sector regulatory institutions and decisions underlying economic policy-making which still assume that the market is as healthy as it was say twenty years ago.

One ironic episode of the public sector's lag concerns itself with the price controls used at one point during the Nixon Administration's New Economic Program (NEP). Whatever the arguments for or against controls, should a government employ them, then the chief question is whether they can contain inflation in the short run. It is now a matter of record that controls worked both during World War II and the Korean War periods. They did not succeed in the 1971 attempt. One reason for this unsuccessful attempt, as Robert Lanzillotti, a former NEP price commissioner has written, was the simple fact that the administration chose to enforce price controls over a vast number of transactions with a miniscule staff of 300 people, less than 10 percent of whom were trained economists. A second reason deals with the current large degree of intracorporate nonmarket transactions of U.S. exports and imports compared to the earlier periods of price controls. The Nixon controls did not take this structural change into account. Thus not controlled was the phenomenon of domestic produced goods transacted on paper as exports to foreign subsidiaries and then again transacted on paper as imports back into the U.S. Since controls did not extend to imports, there were in effect no controls over these types of goods produced and consumed in the U.S. The evidence suggests the phenomenon was widespread in important "linkage" industries like construction materials, semi-processed and processed metals, fertilizers, and agribusiness.

NATIONAL POLICY AND FINANCIAL STRUCTURES

Another major characteristic of the postwar large corporation is the change in the manner by which it finances its expansion across industries and nations. The sheer pace and quantitative magnitude of expansion have necessitated that global enterprises shift significantly their basis of financing from internal to external sources. This shift was accelerated by governmental capital restrictions such as the U.S. voluntary and mandatory balance of payments program. The latter, of course, was a catalyst to the development of the Euro-currency market, a further important structural characteristic of the new pattern of corporate financing and to be discussed immediately below. In addition, the growth of output from this rapid expansion could not be absorbed given actual increases in consumer incomes. Corporations reacted, particularly in consumer durables, through the establishment of ancillary credit-mechanisms and advertising, emphasizing the use of credit, a marketing strategy pointedly and successfully aimed at changing the psychology and propensities of consumers to incur record-breaking debt increases over increases in current income. National governments correspondingly have provided the liquidity to meet the financing needs of this form of expansion, bringing about historic increases in the money supply. This took place at a time when other new structural characteristics of finance (*e.g.*, credit cards, "checking-plus," leasing) have contributed further to unprecedented increases in debt and the velocity of money.

From the perspective of current short-run stabilization policy, however, the Euro-currency market is one of the most important structural innovations of the post-World War II period. Global banks' justifiable and understandable creation of the Euro-currency market to meet the needs of global corporate expansion nevertheless was permitted by national governments to evolve without normal public regulatory control. The latter is perhaps one of the most notable indicators of the structural lag between the public sector's regulatory function and a now transformed private corporate sector. The lack of deposit reserve requirements, particularly, had made this $100 billion-plus pool of deposits an incalculable and unpredictable source of further increases to the world money supply. A second characteristic of the Euro-currency market is that U.S. and other global banks operating within its domain regularly violate the first principle of sound banking: never borrow short to lend long. These aspects of the Euro-currency market have led observers like

Harvard's Professor H. S. Houthakker to note its impact as a "huge creation of private international liquidity," and in his view, "almost certainly contributes powerfully to the inflationary pressures that no nation has succeeded in keeping under control."

Finally, the intracorporate, nonmarket basis of much cross-nation financial flows, the development of an accounting technology for global optimization of firms' liquid assets, combined with the sheer magnitude and rapidity (relative to the past) of these financial transfers has eroded the autonomy or sovereignty of a nation's money supply, implying the increasing inability of national authorities to control it. "Leads and lags," for example, is a standard tool of business, invented long before the age of global companies, to preserve the value of liquid assets during periods of foreign exchange instability. Central bank procedures to account for the effect of leads and lags on the domestic money supply are also age-old. But today, given systemic increases in global concentration and improved accounting technology, these same procedures cannot match the more massive and more rapid liquid transfers by many fewer actors than could have been foreseen a few short years ago.

Leads and lags immediately affect the money supply of a country, yet since they are unrecorded transactions, reflected only in the "errors and omissions" component of a nation's balance of payments account, their actual impact on changing the money stock is discovered by central bankers only after considerable delay. The German experience of the late 1960s and early 1970s illustrates the problem and adds a further reason why current monetary policy has become an unreliable tool for regulating the economy. Studies of the German Bundesbank have found that although its policy led to "complete neutralization of the liquidity inflows to domestic banks," however, "it does not curb the expansive effects exerted by the inflows of funds from abroad to non-banks on the money stock." [2] Additional work on these non-bank inflows by

[2] *Monthly Report of the Deutsche Bundesbank*, March 1973, p. 3; see also Samuel I. Katz, "'Imported Inflation' and the Balance of Payments," New York University, Graduate School of Business Administration, Institute of Finance, *The Bulletin*, nos. 91–92, October 1973.

Michael Porter and published in the *IMF Staff Papers* showed that the Bundesbank's required reserves policies to control the money supply "were substantially and rapidly offset in their effect on bank liquidity by capital inflows recorded mainly in errors and omissions . . . within one month and by some 80 percent."

This example of the loss of sovereignty over the money supply by national governments is also reflected in the 1968-early 1969 episode involving the Federal Reserve Board, U.S. global banks, and the Euro-currency market. The latter two in combination with U.S. global firms has led to what IMF consultant Frank Tamanga has called the "convergence of U.S. multinational corporations and multinational banks into an integrated U.S. economy in exile." This episode involves the attempt to constrain money supply growth by lowering interest rates on certificates of deposit (CDs) with the hope of absorbing these released monies into treasury bills. Instead, these monies were drawn to the higher interest rates of the Euro-currency market. Overnight these liquid assets were brought back into the U.S. by the intrabank borrowings of global banks from their overseas branches. The U.S.-based parent banks in turn used these borrowed deposits to create additional loans to their largest industrial clients, which, for reasons mentioned earlier, were not deterred by the significantly higher interest costs involved. The then low fractional reserve requirements on borrowed Euro-deposits yielded an actual expansion in the U.S. money supply, the exact opposite of the CD-interest policy's intended result. Here we see how the twin forces of globalization and concentration structurally erode the efficacy of the nation-state's aggregate stabilization tools. Although in late 1969 (and again in early 1971), fractional reserve requirements were increased, the inflationary damage had already been done.[3]

---

[3] Even in 1973 after further adjustments by the Federal Reserve Board, financial analysts were still worried over the gap and uncertainty of monetary policy fully "to integrate into its decision-making apparatus the most dynamic and expanding aspect of American banking, the foreign branch operations." See Frank Mastrapasqua, "U.S. Bank Expansion Via Foreign Branching: Monetary Policy Implications," New York University, Graduate School of Business Administration, Institute of Finance, *The Bulletin*, nos. 87–88, January 1973.

MOBILITY VS. IMMOBILITY: THE INFORMATION CRISIS

The capstone characteristic of what Professor Scott Gordon, writing in the *Journal of Political Economy*, has called "one of the most momentous facts of the modern age, the emergence of the corporation as a primary *social* institution" is the structural mobility of this social institution as compared to other primary institutions of our society. As the classical economists from Smith to Schumpeter used the term, structure refers not only to the physical but also to the behavioral aspects of institutions. What distinguishes the global corporation of today from its prewar predecessor is its heightened structural mobility, *i.e.*, its increased capacity to change rapidly where and what it produces, and an accelerating change in its managerial techniques for controlling that production. And what distinguishes the global corporation from other social institutions is that the latter are relatively immobile in the physical sense and much slower to adapt or change in the behavioral sense. Thus, for example, government, national business firms, and organized labor are globally immobile, being largely constrained in their institutional jurisdiction to the home nation.

This theme of mobility versus immobility characterizing the structural lag of the noncorporate institutions of the economy has as a major symptom a "crisis in information." That is, information once provided via the workings of the market is today increasingly either missing or unreliable. For the foreign sector, large-scale corporate sampling surveys reveal over 50 percent of total trade transactions are now of the nonmarket intracorporate variety. Yet official corporate disclosure information requirements of the government can account for only about half this number. The use of intraconglomerate transfers and the advent of such substitute financing as leasing, combined with the growth mentality of the 1960s, has led Leonard Spacek, former chairman of Arthur Andersen & Company, to comment that the words "generally accepted accounting principles" on corporate consolidated balance sheets are a "fiction." He says, "My profession appears to regard a set of financial statements as a roulette wheel." David Norr of the

American Institute of Certified Public Accounting agrees, "Accounting today permits a shaping of results to attain a desired end. Accounting as a mirror of (economic) activity is dead."

Whatever legitimate corporate reasons consolidated balance sheets may serve, from the objective of social purposes, however, they now hide more than they reveal. For instance, a growing number of university studies are now documenting the frustration of unions to make, as a basis of their wage demands, an accurate assessment of the profitability of the particular subsidiary with which they are negotiating since profits may have been shifted to another part of the parent conglomerate's system. For government policy-making, reported corporate trade flows, profits, and debt burdens are the basis of decisions for managing employment, price, and balance of payments stability. But when the statistical basis of these decisions is unreliable and/or misleading then the outcome of policy is, at best, uncertain, at worst, perverse.

These behavioral aspects are not the only characteristics of the new corporate mobility. There is also the physical dimension. In the 1960s, the pace of global oligopoly competition accelerated with the full-fledged entry of European and Japanese enterprises. Driven by international comparative cost differences in first labor and later in tax and anti-pollution costs, American companies offset declining domestic and export market shares by a remarkable mobility in transferring their production facilities to "export platform" facilities in underdeveloped countries. What Boston University's Dean of Business, Peter Gabriel, has termed the "herd instinct" of global corporations showed itself dramatically as the latecomer Japanese and Europeans began to duplicate export platform foreign investments of the pioneer American companies. This pattern, starting in labor intensive industries and quickly shifting to more capital intensive sectors, further reinforced the global interdependence of nations while adding new forms of structural lags and tensions in the home countries. Unions found another aspect of their countervailing power eroded as the threat of strike was effectively offset by the threat of production transfer overseas. Smaller domestic subcontracting firms also felt the impacts of these transfers. In addition, government adjustment assistance programs, designed for times past, are ineffective in correcting the significant regional and industry dislocations in employment and small businesses. While no economist has yet to demonstrate the overall domestic short-term employment impacts, positive or negative, of the new patterns of foreign investment, the results of structural long-term trend analysis are more pessimistic.

In the static, theoretical market world of orthodox economics, changes in international comparative costs, dictating changes in the composition of national output and world trade, should lead to a new equilibrium situation via a path of smooth and rapid adjustments. This model underlying our current policies of course has to assume that factors like labor are mobile and that basic economic institutions like the market and the corporation never significantly change their behavioral characteristics. The real world of imperfect and nonexistent markets, global profit maximization and oligopoly competition, labor and governmental immobility, compounded by rapid changes in certain institutions and none in others, all make, however, for an actual conclusion far removed from that of orthodox theory.

The Dilemma of National Policy-Making

As this is being written, the depths of structural lag in national stabilization policies are profound. Policy-makers have yet to comprehend the many interrelated and intersecting forces arising out of the globalization and concentration processes of the corporate private sector. The worldwide complementary planning decisions of global banks and industrial companies have brought with them a convergence or harmonization in the business cycles of advanced nations. The upshot is that no longer can the U.S. rely, through foreign trade and finance multipliers, on Europe's upswing toward a boom to help bring us out of the declining phase of our own cycle, and vice-versa. Today, one nation's deflationary or inflationary surges help bring about and accelerate those of other countries.

The rise of the global bank now finds its impact in the global interdependence between national financial systems and money supplies, with this web of interdependence feeding through unregulated banking transactions of a Euro-currency market. The structural lag accompanying the rise of the first and pioneering post-market global corporations, those of the petroleum sector, has been finally "overcome" on the supply side by a structural phenomenon called OPEC. Yet the lag persists in developing the financial structure to recycle the dramatic new distribution of worldwide liquid assets which results from the rapid shift in *real* terms of trade arising out of OPEC and like phenomena. And within this matrix of interdependence stands the obvious lag of no global central bank of last resort to stem the now recognized threat of an international spiral of debt liquidation crises triggered through the Euro-currency market.

For those who have been studying the interdependent *structural* changes occurring from the globalization of that "primary social institution," the large corporation, the current economic instability was predictable. For orthodox economists and, unfortunately, the managers and government policy-makers they advise, their preoccupation with *functional* study of changes in aggregate data, using a model that assumes that primary institutions are static, the current events of the day have come as a surprise. The former group analyzes changes in *terms of trade* within sectors of, and between national economies based on changing power relations arising out of the diffusion of new "knowledge" and as functionally constrained at the limits by aggregate supply and demand conditions. The latter group attempts to analyze terms of trade by a functional focus on supply and demand with little regard for changing power relations between primary institutions. The structuralist model incorporates the functional approach. The functionalist model sees as unnecessary, and thereby assumes away, the study of structural changes. Surrounding a period of structural transformation the current functional model breaks down and so too the efficacy of its policy prescriptions. At this point the model needs "updating" to bring it closer to the structural reality within which it seeks to predict. So it was with Keynes, who, in the midst of the crisis in economics of the 1930s, built upon the work of the Swedish structuralism-functionalism school of Wicksell and Myrdal to derive a new model for policy-making purposes, operative until the next, and in this case our current, period of structural transformation. The present crisis in economics was well summarized by former Secretary of the Treasury, George Shultz: "We have come into a very unusual period, where we more or less cast loose from beliefs that we once held to be unarguable. We have cast off from a large number of these old moorings and we have not yet found new ones."

There is neither space left, nor is this the place for detailed proposals for dealing with the inefficacy of current national stabilization policies. The summary conclusions of this analysis do permit us, however, to point to the chief parameters which will govern policy approaches to the problems of contemporary economic instability. This analysis' overall conclusion states that the traditionally accepted public sector regulatory institutions for managing the economy are structurally lagging behind the revolution in the basic institutions of the private sector. The most notable symptom of this structural lag is an information crisis due to the mutually reinforcing processes of corporate globalization and concentration as they negate the market's social *function* for providing a reliable guide to policy-making. An additional aspect of this conclusion is that the ultimate result of corporate globalization has been the obviously greatly increased degree in interdependence between nation-states. But the political implication of this interdependence is yet to be sufficiently understood.

On the one hand, there is in fact a clear need in the U.S. to ask fundamental questions about the adequacy of current public regulatory institutions like antitrust laws, corporate disclosure laws, accounting conventions, banking, and labor relations legislation, and the tax base itself of the government. On the other hand, such seemingly national political issues have unpredictable economic impacts in a time of global interdependence. Thus, the modification by only one nation-state of the public sector's regulatory function is severely limited unless such modifications are harmonized among all advanced countries. This is true because of the nature of global oligopoly competition and the extent to which national income is now dependent on the competitiveness of home nation global corporations in their overseas operations. If the regulatory institutions of only one country are modified in an attempt to provide more reliable stabilization policies, there is a distinct probability that this nation's national income will suffer. In this case competitive oligopoly advantages could well accrue to the global corporations of other nations.

Thus the age old dilemma of the oligopolist—"If I do not take advantage of an opportunity my competitors will"—becomes, in an era of global interdependence and corporations, the dilemma of the national policy-maker, and the underlying rationale for international harmonization. Nation-states, however, have different comparative resource endowments, different levels of development and developmental goals and, therefore, different national interests. It is within this context that the politics of international harmonization will have to deal with what, in the opinion of this writer, undoubtedly will be basic institutional modifications if world economic stability is to be regained. Whether or not global harmonization is politically feasible and, if so, for whom it will be economically desirable, is, of course, the prime issue of the national and international "econopolitics" of the years ahead.

Seymour J. Rubin

4

The Multinational Enterprise
and the "Home" State

In their operations multinational companies from time to time find themselves at cross-purposes not only with the governments of the nations in which they are doing business but also with the government of the state in which they are domiciled. The effort has been made in this book to examine both sets of relations, to isolate the areas of conflict, and to suggest possible means of reconciliation. The following chapter deals with the relations of the multinational corporation and its "home" state.

G. W. B.

However it may be defined, the multinational enterprise is agreed to be an important and growing actor on the world stage. Terminology differs: what is to some the transnational company is to others the international corporation or the multinational enter-

SEYMOUR J. RUBIN *is Professor of Law at American University in Washington, D.C., as well as counsel to a private law firm. He is a member of the International Juridical Committee, the legal body of the Organization of American States, and has been Assistant Director of the Mutual Security Administration, General Counsel of A.I.D., and U.S. Representative at the Development Assistance Committee and the U.N. Commission on International Trade Law. His books include* Private Foreign Investment *and* The Conscience of the Rich Nations, *and he was editor of and contributor to* Foreign Development Lending—Legal Aspects *(1971).*

prise. But the phenomenon of the corporation which is incorporated in one nation, in which its principal control resides, with producing affiliates, either incorporated or not, in other nations, has flourished, especially in the decades since World War II. To such an extent has this happened, and to such an extent has trade between companies affiliated under the umbrella of the multinational increased, that it has been suggested that "international firms have now taken over, and there is every indication that international business is now the dominant factor in determining changes in the pattern of world exports as well as capital flows."

The consequences of this development have been viewed in various ways. Galbraith has suggested that the consequence is a system which "internationalizes the tendency to inequality." Many have enunciated the fear of Servan-Schreiber that, "The sheer power of these economic giants has out-stripped the ability of states to control them." Others, like Arnold Toynbee, consider that fact, if it be a fact, to be a desirable result: the nation-state is regarded by Toynbee as a threat to the very survival of civilization. In the developing nations as a whole, and perhaps most articulately in the nations of Latin America, the reaction has been other. In defense of national sovereignty, the writers and to some extent the legislators of such nations have advocated or enacted a series of measures: increasingly stringent entry requirements; "fade-out" requirements; denial of such benefits as may come from tariff reductions or elimination among the nations of customs unions like the Andean Pact; and limitations on royalty payments.

Other writers have described the benefits brought to the world, including the developing world, by the multinationals: the flow of capital into needy economies; the accompanying flow of technology; the betterment of economic and of social conditions, as production rose, as jobs grew, as real wages increased, and so forth. In rebuttal, it has been charged that the multinationals have led the developing nations into an undesirable consumerism; that they have been pushed into production suited to the multinationals' best interest, not to their own; that the technology has been purchased too dearly, and on a basis which condemns the developing nation to a perpetual state of payment and of technological inferiority; and that the flow of capital is, in reality and on balance, out of, rather than into, the developing nations.

The size of the multinationals and the extent of their resources give rise to fears that their actions may override the policies of home and host nations alike. The charge is thus made that during the recent series of monetary crises, a substantial part of the disequilibrium was produced by the "sloshing" of corporate funds from one currency to another, as corporate controllers sought to beat the devaluation of one currency or the appreciation of another. In the tax area, it is suggested, the multinational may pay duty to no one. The frequent tributes to private foreign investment, or to the multinationals, in such international documents as the "Action Programme of the General Assembly for the Second United Nations Development Decade" thus sound more like formal and ritualistic expressions than deeply felt sentiments.

Traditionally, it has been the less developed nations—or those pressing their cause—which have argued the iniquities rather than the benefits of the multinationals. But in recent years, at least two other voices have been added to the chorus of criticism: that of developed nations, which fear the frustration of their polity by multinationals, with consequences unfavorable to their ability to determine that polity; and home nation groups, which have blamed the multinational for the export of capital which might better have stayed at home, and for sending technology abroad, at bargain rates, to the detriment of home nation jobs and work standards.

In its relations with its home nation, the multinational is several not entirely consistent beings.

It is, in the first instance, a vehicle—a conduit by which home nation policies may be transmitted to other parts of the world. Limited though this power clearly is, and doubtful though may be the legal implications which it carries with it, it implies an important aspect of the relationship between the multinational and the home state. This ability to function as a conduit is something of which other nations are equally aware, and to which they may well be extremely sensitive.

Secondly, there is the aspect of the multinational which is expressed in the aphorism that the flag follows commerce. Many, if not most, of the disputes between the United States and the nations of Latin America, for example, are investment disputes—the attempt by the United States to assist an American national—generally but not always corporate—to obtain what it, and the United States by endorsing its claim, consider to be fair treatment abroad. One need not invoke the simplistic notion that big government is the tool of big business to have some thoughts, and perhaps worries, about the process that leads a government to find a foreign policy issue in an investment which is made for private reasons. The question occurs whether the government should be in on the take-off if it is in on the crash.

Third, the size, the capacities, and the flexibility of at least some multinational enterprises raise the question of whether they can be controlled by national governments, either home or host. In many situations, the so-called multinational enterprise does not in fact have much flexibility. If, for example, it has invested abroad in order to obtain essential supplies—the typical situation in the extractive industries—its options may be very limited. If its purpose in going abroad has been to capture or retain a foreign market, again limitations are imposed by the requirements of that objective. But when it can produce components or finished products as well in one nation as in another, serious issues of control are posed. To what extent can such a corporation, by shifting the locale of all or part of its activities evade the strictures of the policy of home or host nation? To what extent can the determinant of its actions be its own decisions as to what is in its corporate—and de-nationalized—interest? Does such a multinational have such power that the ability of *any* single nation-state to control it has been left far behind? These issues, which are somewhat beyond the scope of a discussion of "home" state–multinational enterprise relationships, involve the long-range political and economic role of the multinational enterprise and ought to be kept in mind in any such discussion.

The Multinational as Conduit: Extraterritoriality

The issue of extraterritoriality—the asserted tendency of the home state to extend its jurisdiction into the territory of a foreign state—is almost exclusively an American problem. There are two reasons for this: the American-based multinational is still, despite a growing multinationalization of the multinational enterprise, far and away dominant; and the United States, more than any other "capitalistic" or "nonsocialistic" economy, covers the business activities of its citizens with a web of regulation and prescription.

From the point of view of size, and nature of activities, United States-based multinationals would seem to provide a broad avenue for the transmission of policy. American multinationals are active in the entire range of industry, from the extractive industries to manufacture—including dominance in some areas of the latter, such as the field of computer technology. The American multinational bank leads the way in financing the industrial multinationals. In the developing nations, American business multinationals account for one-half of the total stock of foreign direct investment; for Central and South America, the figure is two-thirds. In the Middle East, United States investment is 57 percent of the total; in Asia, 36 percent; and in Africa, some 20 percent. For certain nations, the figures are even higher: the 1968 figures for Chile, Colombia, Panama, Peru, the Philippines, and Saudi Arabia showed American affiliates owning over 80 percent of the stock of foreign investment. More than half of the multinationals with total annual sales of manufactures in excess of one billion dollars are American, and more than half of the total estimated book value of foreign investment in 1971 of about $160 billion was associated with United States-based companies.

The very large size and number of the American-based multinationals occasion particular concern because of a somewhat special aspect of American regulatory policy. Regulation in the United States is extensive. The bulk of such regulation has, of course, only domestic implications: legislation with respect to wages and hours, or with respect to fair selling practices, normally applies only internally. But some such legislation affects the external actions of the American national—individual or corporate—and some such actions are regarded as being within the jurisdiction of nations other than the United States. The broad sweep of such legislation, combined with a latitudinarian definition of the extent of American jurisdiction, has given rise to the charge that the American-based multinational enterprise is a conduit for the extension of American policy into nations which regard that extension as a violation of their own jealously-guarded sovereignty.

The problem—roughly defined as that of extraterritoriality—arises typically in a few situations.

ANTITRUST LEGISLATION

A major concern of the United States—or indeed any other home nation—is that the foreign operations of home-based international business not result in frustration of domestic laws or regulations. Since 1890, when the Sherman Act was enacted, it has been the law of the United States that "every contract, combination . . . or conspiracy in restraint of trade or commerce among the several States, *or with foreign nations* . . ." is illegal (emphasis added). That policy has been reaffirmed and amplified several times—in the Wilson Tariff Act of 1894, and in the Clayton and Federal Trade Commission Acts. The Clayton Act specifically prohibits enterprises subject to United States jurisdiction from any acquisitions the effects of which "may be substantially to lessen competition or to tend to create a monopoly."

Under this broad language, acts done abroad may bring an American corporation into conflict with the law. Foreign acquisitions for example may seriously diminish sources of competitive imports, or may put an American company into a position of undesirable dominance over its rivals. Nonetheless, the initial interpretation of the United States Supreme Court was to give the Sherman Act effect only as to acts done in the United States; and the American Banana case, decided in 1909 in an opinion by Mr. Justice Holmes, went on the ground that it could not have been the intent of Congress to make criminal acts which had occurred on foreign soil, and were legal under the law of the nation in which they took place.

That early interpretation has long since been overruled, in substance if not in explicit words. In 1945, in the Alcoa case, Judge Learned Hand pronounced what is now settled doctrine: ". . . that any state may impose liabilities, even upon persons not within its allegiance, for conduct outside its borders that has consequences within its borders that the state reprehends." This doctrine, the so-called "effects" doctrine of jurisdiction, has consistently since then been applied by the United States, in the field of antitrust, and in other areas to which it is relevant. It is now enshrined in the semi-authoritative restatement of the Foreign Relations Law of the United States.

The immediate consequences of application of this doctrine have been a series of clashes between United States policy and that of other nations, in which the corporation has on occasion been something like the bird in a badminton game. For example, the Imperials Chemicals-Dupont case, which occupied the time of the courts on both sides of the Atlantic in the early 1950s, featured a tug-of-war between the prohibition of conduct in the United States and the enforcement of that same conduct in Britain. In a somewhat similar situation, the Swiss government strongly protested the application of the decree of an American court which had been based on the thesis that jurisdiction existed if "acts and contracts have a substantial and material effect upon our foreign and domestic commerce."

What has been the effect of these and other cases on the relations of the American-based multinational with its home, and with its host, governments?

Insofar as relations with the host nations are concerned it is safe to venture the guess that there has been little direct criticism of the corporation itself. In every case, by definition, the multinational enterprise has been prevented by the United States from taking action which it desires, and which the host government either encourages or condones. One may imagine, thus, that the corporate manager and the host are in accord in deploring the controverted prohibitions.

It is, indeed, the application of U.S. policy within a foreign nation, via the multinational, that is most criticized. Too much should not be made of such criticism, for the scope of conflict has over the years been much reduced. European antitrust policies, under the developing doctrines of Articles 85 and 86 of the Treaty of Rome, have grown to be remarkably similar to those of the United States. Indeed, the European Economic Community has itself had its crisis of extraterritoriality over enforcement of one of its antitrust decrees. And consultative devices—within the framework of a special Canadian-United States agreement, and within the framework of the OECD—have taken the bite out of what promised at one time to become a bitterly controverted subject. Indeed, in the course of a critique of the issue of extraterritoriality in Canada, the latest official Canadian report remarks mildly that

> Historically, the impact of United States antitrust law on Canadian industry has not been serious. There are only a few cases in which the United States decrees affected Canadian activities—and their economic impact has probably been beneficial in increasing Canadian industrial efficiency.

Nonetheless problems remain, which arise out of the fact that the American-based enterprise is subject to United States antitrust law. The legal relationship with the home government may be determinative of the business decisions of the enterprise; and those decisions—whether properly described as extraterritorial or not—can substantially affect economic decision-making within the host nation. To take an example: if an American and a Canadian corporation with similar product lines decide to form a joint venture in Canada, that venture might be viewed as a means of limiting exports to the United States from a previously independent Canadian competitor. The result may be, as the 1972 Canadian Report states, that

> a bias exists in the law for United States firms to establish wholly owned subsidiaries in Canada. Such subsidiaries run fewer risks of being accused of eliminating or limiting exports to Canada in cooperation with a Canadian company or of restricting exports from Canada to the United States of otherwise independent business units.

Harmonization of antitrust policy seems to be taking place to some extent, but doctrinal differences remain. Even within the Common Market of Europe, rationalization of industry appears to be as much an objective as is the competitive model. As to antitrust, Japan presents another contrast in philosophy with the United

States. Under these circumstances, and even with consultative procedures reducing the judicial conflicts, the likelihood is that the relationship of the home government with the multinational will be a cause for suspicion. That the multinational may dislike the embrace of its own government as much as does the host nation will, in these circumstances, not greatly ease tensions. It will nonetheless, under compulsion or not, be regarded as tailoring its economic policies in the host nation to the realities of its potential liabilities to the home government.

THE TRADING WITH THE ENEMY ACT: EXPORT CONTROLS

The United States has long regulated trade between United States nationals and entities abroad. And from the very beginnings of the nation, discretionary power to impose or to lift controls over such commerce has been delegated by the Congress to the President, who in turn has passed it on to one or another of the Executive departments. In the case of The Brig *Aurora*, in 1813, the Supreme Court upheld this delegation. In the situation of export controls, the President (or his designee) exercises authority, insofar as the foreign operations of American affiliates are concerned, under the Trading with the Enemy Act, supplemented importantly by various statutes which regulate the export of technology from the United States, under which restrictions on the use or re-export of such technology are imposed.

It is, in the main, the Trading with the Enemy Act and its administration which have most acutely raised, at home and abroad, the issue of the relation of the multinational with its home government, and the consequent extension of home government policies into the decisions of foreign, host, nations. And clearly this is the most visible, and most resented, aspect of the extraterritoriality which arises from the authority of the United States over "its" multinationals. The use by the home government to transmit its undesired policies to the host nation via the multinational has resulted in strident protest. Refusal in early 1974 to permit American subsidiaries, incorporated in Canada and in Argentina, and therefore "nationals" of those nations, to export to Cuba brought on such clamor that the United States relaxed the prohibitions imposed under the Trading with the Enemy Act. One may speculate whether there was any increase of resentment against the American firms; after all, the companies themselves were as aggrieved by the denials as were the host nations. It may be supposed, however, that the scrutiny of host nations of a proposed new investment is intensified, and the attitude of the host government somewhat less receptive, when there is such a demonstration, so evocative of feelings of outraged nationalism, of the utility of the multinational as a chain of transmission of home nation polity.

The two American statutes which most importantly control the activities of subsidiaries abroad are the Export Administration Act and the Trading with the Enemy Act. Under the first, licenses of different sorts are required for the export from the United States of technical data and commodities. Most such exports are made pursuant to "general licenses," which in effect permit the free export to most nations of most commodities. Some materials and data, mainly in the field of so-called strategic items, are more tightly controlled; and some nations are subject to restrictions of varying degrees of severity.

As to exports from the United States, no complaint of extraterritoriality can be made. But when goods are exported to, say, Canada, the same restrictions are imposed for re-export as would be applicable for direct export from the United States. Moreover, the United States follows components and technical data through the processes of assembly and manufacture abroad with the same restrictions. Such restrictions are binding on any person, of whatever nationality. As to an American citizen, penalties of several sorts may be imposed; as to foreign nationals, denial of export privileges from the United States may follow violation of these restrictions.

The difficulty here arises in the situation in which the foreign nation has its own concepts of what are or are not strategic materials, and when those differ from the views held in Washington. In such circumstances the nation in which a product is assembled or manufactured may regard that product, despite inclusion of some non-national components, as being essentially national in origin, and may well allow—perhaps even direct—its export to destinations prohibited by the United States. Thus, in a nation like Canada, dependent very largely on American technology and goods, with an enormous number of plants owned by, and therefore likely to import components from American-based parent companies, there is substantial scope for complaint that Canadian policy is being made in Washington rather than in Ottawa. This is despite the existence of an informal grouping of NATO nations and Japan which seeks to coordinate policies and definitions applicable to export of strategic materials to the "Sino-Soviet bloc" (a term which, though still used, seems in the seventies curiously anachronistic).

The controls under the Trading with the Enemy Act are even more controversial. Since those controls apply to "any person" over whom the United States has jurisdiction, and since the boards of directors of many foreign subsidiaries of American corporations are composed in whole or part of American citizens, the potential scope of application of these controls is very wide. Conflict has resulted. The classic case was that of Fruehauf-France, a French subsidiary of an American company. Fruehauf-France signed a contract with another French company (Berliet) to sell to it equipment intended to be incorporated into trucks which Berliet was then to export to the Peoples Republic of China. The U.S. Treasury, using the authority of the Trading with the Enemy Act, ordered the American parent to order its French subsidiary to break the Berliet contract. Berliet having asserted its rights and threatened suit, the minority French directors of Fruehauf-France went to court. They argued that they were bound to the contract under French law; that damages would be assessed against them were the contract to be broken; and that injury would thus be caused to French stockholders of Fruehauf-France. The court, in what has become an exemplar of the ability of the host nation to control, installed a receiver in the company long enough to ensure that the contract was fulfilled—after which the company was turned back to management.

It can well be argued that neither the Export Administration Act nor the Trading with the Enemy Act result in confrontations like those here described with any frequency; that American policy is softening, with the consequence that conflicts of policy are fewer than before; and that the issue is not one which necessarily implicates multinationals or foreign investment, since the United States can use denial of its technology or commodities to impose—if the price is right—its will on *any* foreign purchaser, subsidiary, or independent. But the argument avoids the problem of a dramatic and open use, in the main, of the American-based multinational as the vehicle for imposition of undesired foreign trading policies on a sovereign nation. Even when, as has several times happened in application of controls to Canada, consultation has resulted in U.S. permission to carry out the questioned transaction, the need for a grant of such permission emphasizes the dependence of an economy such as that of Canada on the United States, and exacerbates tensions already at a high level. Equally important is the suspicion that the will of the United States, rather than that of the host nation, like Canada, is done in a multitude of unperceived and undetectable situations. One cannot know how many export opportunities have been lost to Canadian subsidiaries of American firms because their directors knew that a question would be raised, and therefore avoided the problems by not promoting or seeking trade which might be queried by Washington.

The behavior of affiliated companies is likely to be affected by their affiliation, by the fact that they are part of a multinational enterprise with, at least in the overall, common objectives. Subsidiaries are not likely to be independent of the interests of their parent corporations. The economy of the United States is very far from the ideal of a free enterprise economy; given the vast interrelations between industry and government, it is a mixed economy, in which many industries are dependent on a wide variety of governmental decisions. These may range from the question of a subsidy to a depressed industry to issues of tax or of renegotiation of profits to contractual relations which are vital to the "private" enterprise. In such circumstances, it would seem plausible that a parent corporation in the United States—and no less in other home nations, perhaps more—would transmit when it could, to foreign affiliates, even the unspoken but easily inferred desires of the government with which it has such relations.

A possible response may be that it is not that easy to infer governmental suggestions, that policy, in Washington as in other capitals, is itself ill-defined, and is a shifting compromise between the views of competing governmental interests. The American-based multinational may, therefore, not be able to ascertain with certainty just what is the policy of the United States, and consequently will be unable to act as a vehicle of that policy. Assuming the validity of that somewhat rueful proposition, it does not commend itself as an adequate response to complaints based on the ability of the home government to extend its writ, when it can in fact decide just what it does desire, to foreign affiliates.

IMPACT AND EFFECTS

An examination of the home-host relationship in the areas of antitrust and of export controls indicates that the laws and policies of one state may be extended abroad even in situations in which there does not exist the corporate familial relationship of the multinational or transnational company. A firm in Italy may be required not to incorporate helicopter technology gained under license from an American firm unless it agrees to abide by United States government decisions as to destinations for the helicopters which it produces. In such an instance, corporate affiliation is as much beside the point as it is in the case of cartel arrangements between two companies which are entirely independent except in their common desire to allocate markets.

A corporate affiliation, however, enlarges both the means and the likelihood that there will be an imposition of the will of the one nation into the affairs of the other. It may at least parenthetically here be noted that such an effect is in many cases entirely defensible; it can hardly be surprising that if direct export of strategic materials to certain nations is prohibited, the prohibiting nation will consider it undesirable to do by simple indirection what is forbidden to do directly. Nonetheless, corporate affiliation opens up a broad channel. It therefore comes under more intense, and often more hostile, examination, than does, for example, the attempted application of an antitrust decree to independent entities.

Possibilities exist between components of a corporate system which are not otherwise available. For example, the home government may, in times of balance of payment difficulties, direct its companies to repatriate profits from their foreign subsidiaries. The benefit to the home state may be matched by a detriment to the host. In any case, the possibility—which depends on the existence of the multinational enterprise—creates an understandable unease in host nations, and especially in a nation like Canada, with its enormous amount of American-affiliated commerce and industry.

In addition to making easier the transmission process, the existence of the multinational company may vastly broaden the scope of decisions made outside the host jurisdiction. Here one comes to the point sketched above: that often not to do something is as much a decision as to act affirmatively. The literature in the field of "extraterritoriality" tends to focus on the dramatic cases of conflicts of will, which almost always begin with an explicit and visible command—as, in the Fruehauf-France case, to break a contract with another company. Little attention has been paid to the situations in which it is not necessary to reconcile conflicts, in Foreign Office consultations, in the chambers of the OECD, or elsewhere, because the situations which led to the necessity to reconcile conflicts are not permitted to develop. These are the cases in which the business which might cause problems is just not sought—the foreign subsidiaries of American companies which have not created a confrontation on, for example, trade with Cuba, because they have not cultivated or have quietly avoided opportunities for such trade.

It may be, thus, that the situations which find their way into the casebooks and the headlines have diverted attention from more important realities. Where the internation corporate relationships may have their major application in the extension overseas of home nation policy is probably in the unnoticed areas—the contracts not made, the contacts not sought, the exclusion from a range of business options those which the corporate managers feel might give offense at home. Similarly, decisions may be taken, perhaps chiefly for reasons entirely related to the welfare of the company, but influenced not a little by relationships with the home nation. Mr. Dooley said that the Supreme Court follows the elections; and it would be surprising if, following the introduction of the Burke-Hartke proposals, companies which had an option to establish a plant at home or one abroad did not feel that the choice of the foreign site would have been unwise.

The Multinational Enterprise and the Flag

Typically, the multinational enterprise owns property abroad (generally indirectly, via a foreign-incorporated subsidiary) which is used in production. Discussion of "the problem" of the multinational has tended to concentrate on the issues surrounding production and sale—the business activities of the enterprise. It is here that debate has raged. Do the multinationals produce a total world benefit? Do they induce a consumption psychology especially in the developing nations which is detrimental to the social and economic progress of the majority of the people of the world? Do they restrict rather than encourage the transfer of a technology suitable to relevant progress? Does their presence repress and restrict the development of a competitive and efficient domestic industry? Even if they do produce net benefits on a global basis, are such benefits equitably distributed, as between home and host nation? And do such benefits, when they accrue to the host nation, merely widen existing social disparities and deepen the gulf between the rich and the poor?

There is an aspect of the multinational, and of its relation both to home and to host state, which is inextricably interwoven with these questions of conduct and of operations. That is the issue of the status of property in one nation which is owned by the nationals of another state—the issue of private foreign investment. In one form or another, this issue is a familiar one in the international scene. A classic debate took place in the 1930s, when Secretary of State

Cordell Hull exchanged a series of notes with the Mexican authorities, arising out of the oil and agrarian expropriations. The familiar formulation, often varied in form but never in substance, was then graven in stone, on both sides. On the American side—and, it is fair to say, that of other developed capital-exporting nations—the thesis has been that such property can be taken by the state in which it is located only on the payment of prompt, adequate, and effective compensation. Indeed, there was at one time a thesis that such payment had to be in advance—that title could not pass until the former owner had been satisfied. For the developing countries, the doctrine has been consistently and with even more fervor advanced that no such limitation on the sovereignty of nations exists or ever did exist, and that, while fair treatment is generally guaranteed by the constitutions and statutes of the expropriating nation, the definition of the substance and the form of such treatment is a matter for the unfettered judgment of the nation in which the property was physically located.

To supplement these opposing views, equally opposite procedural theses have been advanced: on the one side, that the nation whose national claimed an unlawful taking had a right to intervene on his behalf, and indeed, to make his claim its own; on the other, that any such intervention implied an unacceptable infusion of government into an investment, the premise of which was its private character. The differences in points of view have been, for the United States and Latin America, epitomized in the discussions of the Calvo Doctrine (the thesis that intervention by a state in an investment dispute is unacceptable) and in the refusal of Latin American nations to accept even the mild commitment to arbitration of such disputes which is embodied in the World Bank's International Center for the Settlement of Investment Disputes.

Except in the situation of very general capital controls, like the now-expired Foreign Direct Investment Control program, or of specific prohibitions (re trade with or investment in Cuba, for example) the United States does not undertake to guide the foreign investments of its nationals. The investor has freedom to make such foreign investment as he chooses. But his decision, under current American doctrine, and except in special circumstances, is also a foreign policy decision of the government. The investor considers that it is a matter of right that he be able to appeal for and obtain the assistance of the government if he can plausibly argue that he is being unfairly treated abroad. More, he can expect, on the basis of ample precedent, that his government will in many cases take up and espouse his claim as if it were that of the government itself. The private investment is wrapped, as it were, in the flag.

Somewhat curiously, this aspect of the multinational corporation has stimulated little basic analysis. It is generally simply accepted that governments will "protect" the overseas investments of their nationals. Debate then centers on methods. A *Wall Street Journal* article of May 1973 on the problem of expropriation risks thus makes the point that "In simpler times, governments had simpler ways of protecting their citizens' private investments in distant lands. The U.S. could send the Marines splashing ashore in Central America, or the British could send swashbuckling generals up the Nile"; and the writer then goes on to discuss the "more civilized and sophisticated methods" which now prevail, such as investment insurance. The assumption of an entitlement to protection is not questioned—despite the long history of international legal debate.

The merits may well be on the side of the traditional United States position, both as a matter of theory and as a matter of sound practice. But the intimate association of the investor—these days mainly the multinational—with his "home" government deserves more than a passing glance.

Since the early days of the Republic, there has been little question that "private" overseas investment was the concern of the state. Perhaps this is because overseas investment was a Crown monopoly, with such great multinationals as the East India Company being granted its charter in 1500 as a special concession of the Crown—and with governmental powers which eventually made that company a formal as well as functioning arm of government. Nations have not hesitated to utilize the foreign holdings of their nationals as their own: the British mobilized the foreign assets of British companies to help pay for World War II; the French did so also, at the insistence of so staunch a conservative as Senator Vandenberg, as a condition of receiving American

Marshall Plan aid. For so many purposes have the private foreign investments of a nation been treated by that nation as a public resource that it is not so surprising as at first glance it would seem that protection has been taken as axiomatic. So much has this been so that George Kennan, in his *Realities of American Foreign Policy*, was able to say that "the assurance of national security and the promotion of American private activity abroad, were all that really did flow directly and logically from the original objects of American society."

If the legitimacy of protecting the foreign investment has been assumed rather than debated, a considerable amount of controversy has surrounded the issue of just how that protection was to be accorded. As already noted, the use of the Marines seems to have gone out of favor, though mutterings about that method have been revived as it has become apparent that the standards of living of a considerable, and formerly confident, part of the world lies in hostage to those who hold sovereignty over the oil sands. Two other methods of protecting the foreign investor have been utilized. One, the method of threatening to withhold favors, has been the basis of various American limitations imposed by the Congress on the granting of concessional aid—from the Kem to the Hickenlooper to the Gonzalez amendments to various foreign aid bills. The other, less clearly an "or else" type of action, has been the investment guaranty—the thesis that private foreign investment both benefits the developing economy and is in the interest of the capital-exporting nations, and that therefore it is to the mutual benefit of the parties on both sides that guaranties against various risks of loss be given to the intrepid investor in useful industry in developing economies.

Of these two methods, that of compulsion has certainly been the more controversial. But controversy surrounds not only the use of this type of compulsion, but even the question whether compulsion is an appropriate description of the method. Why, indeed, should concessional aid be given to a nation whose conduct does not comport with the standards of the "donor"? Few would argue that there is a moral obligation to aid a repressive regime, and thus to bolster its ability to repress—though many might debate whether that principle is properly applied to a Greece of the colonels, or a Rhodesia of Ian Smith, or even a Viet Nam of Thieu. Nonetheless, if concessional aid is withheld from a nation solely because its notion of fairness to a private investor does not satisfy the standards of that investor's home nation, regardless of whether that withholding is justifiable, it becomes obvious that the private business of the multinational corporation/investor has become inextricably intermingled with the public foreign policy of the home nation.

Perhaps the most publicized instance of this kind of correlation between private foreign investment and public policy has been the case of International Petroleum Company, in Peru. In that case, controversy swirled about the issue of violation or not of existing contracts, duress and overreaching in the making of concession agreements, validity or not of claims for taxes reaching back into the early history of the company, and fairness or not of the proffered compensation. The threat of cut-off of United States aid was ever-present. Whether it was an impediment or an assist in the eventual agreement is difficult to assess. That the public policy of the United States, with respect to development assistance and especially in the context of the Alliance for Progress, was engaged in the IPC-Peru dispute is clear.

Insurance for private foreign investment has been another link between the multinational enterprise with its ownership of overseas producing facilities, and the home nation. Though this method of protection involves, at least in the first instance, the investor and his own government, and though any recourse to the host nation depends entirely on such commitments as that nation has made, the insuring government may become deeply enmeshed in political difficulties. In at least one important respect, however, the commitments implied in investment insurance can be consciously limited. Insurance does not necessarily require that the government back up its nationals on any and all of their investments. The Hickenlooper type of approach states that if *any* American investment abroad is taken without arrangements for just compensation being made, American aid shall be terminated. The insurance arrangement would pay the investor if his property is taken (or if other risks materialize); but only those who qualify, in the opinion of the insuring agency—which goes into such questions as the nature of the investment, the needs of the host nation, etc.—are eligible for insurance.

It may thus be argued that the kind of insurance made available to American-based multinationals, or investors, prevents rather than promotes confrontation between home and host nations. Only those investments which meet certain standards are insured; only—it may be inferred—insured investments, at least as among those made after insurance became available, will involve the home government in demands for what it considers to be fair compensation.

Limitations on and objections to this doctrine are immediately apparent. Investment insurance is available only as an adjunct to developmental programs. Should not home nation help be available to the investor who puts his funds into a *developed* economy—say France or Canada—and then is unfairly treated? Or is there an implicit suggestion that it is only the developing nations, not the more developed, which will ever be "unfair"? And does it necessarily follow that the approval of the insuring agency has in fact eliminated the necessity of judging, when the controverted action is taken, whether the public policy of the home nation should be engaged on the side of the private investment? Does insurance merely make certain that every controversy involving an (insured) investment will implicate the home government, and thereby create a virtue out of the intransigence of the investor?

Many of these latter questions have been taken up in the hearings of the Senate Subcommittee on Multinational Corporations, and embodied in its report of October 1973. That report dealt with the Overseas Private Investment Corporation (OPIC), established as a separate government corporation in 1970, and insuring American investors abroad against the risks of inconvertibility, expropriation, and war. The program administered by OPIC had its origins in the Marshall Plan, and the 1948 legislation establishing the Economic Cooperation Administration. It has remained, whether formally a part of the aid program or separately administered, an aspect of development assistance. The rationale is that growth and social progress are concomitant; that an infusion of foreign capital, and the technology accompanying it, contribute to growth; and that a reasonable insurance against those risks which the investor could not reasonably be expected to assume would promote the beneficial flow of capital to the developing nations.

The broad issues—whether guaranties promote investment, whether investment abroad does "promote economic development in its broad definition of social change and economic growth," as the Senate Subcommittee somewhat ambiguously defines them—may be left to one side for purposes of this discussion. What is more to the point is the question of whether the guaranty program involves the home government in controversy with host nations more than would otherwise be the case. And whether the consequent explicit identification of the American-based multinational with American foreign policy is desirable.

The Senate Subcommittee instances three cases—Jamaica, Taiwan, and Chile. It charges that large OPIC exposure to potential losses as a result of its coverage of expropriation risks in those nations had a substantial effect on official United States policy. It cites the American Ambassador in Jamaica in 1970 as testifying that he had been concerned both by the large U.S. financial exposure in Jamaica as a result of OPIC guaranties of bauxite investments, and by the possibility that a refusal of further guaranties might be construed by Jamaica as an implicit statement of no confidence. And it quotes his testimony that he had committed his honor as a gentleman to the leading (and subsequently elected) Presidential candidate that if the bauxite question were kept out of the election campaign "we would not, repeat not, interfere in his elections in any way."

The Taiwanese case is merely that of the possible negative implications of terminating the guaranty program. One could as readily argue that termination of guaranties ought to be read as an expression of confidence, not of lack of confidence. But Chile, with the public exposure of the activities of certain American corporations, and the asserted involvement of the U.S. government, is a more serious matter. Nonetheless, even here, it is unclear whether such involvement as the United States may have had in denial of credits with the intent of bringing down President Allende had any connection whatsoever with guaranties issued by OPIC, or indeed, with the existence of American investment. More likely, such actions as were taken reflect a mixture of very real suspicion that Chile under Allende was in fact not credit-worthy and worries about the political impact of a weak Socialist regime as a breeding ground for political movements throughout Latin America which were considered to be dangerous.

The correctness of the Senate Subcommittee's conclusion—that the program administered by OPIC "tends to increase the likelihood of United States Government involvement in the internal politics of other countries in connection with the property interests of United States corporations"—is doubtful. Other Congressional reports on OPIC suggest the contrary. What does seem evident is that, with or without the guaranties, there is such an involvement. The guaranty program may, as its proponents argue, diminish the risk of unexpected and unwelcome confrontation, rather than increase it. With or without guaranties, the involvement of the home government with its foreign investors is such that, as between home and host nations, the statement of Madison in the tenth number of *The Federalist* may well come to mind: "Those who hold and those who are without property have ever formed distinct interests in society."

Whether the multinational is regarded as the instrument of home state policy or whether its actions implicate and affect the foreign policies of its home nation, issues of international economic and political relations are posed. Appreciation of these issues is desirable if not essential to formulation of an informed and consistent policy, both as to what home states will ask of "their" multinationals and as to what role those states will allow multinationals to play in determination of their foreign policy.

George W. Ball

5

The Relations
of the Multinational Corporation
to the "Host" State

Lawyers are sometimes given to anthropomorphic fancies, and this may well have led to the happy conceit regarding the corporation as a person and citizen as though it might be expected to arise every morning and salute the flag. This should, however, create few problems. Anglo-Saxon institutions have had a habit of developing by the fabrication of fictions that have later shed their pretenses, and sooner or later we shall no doubt get rid of the practice of treating multinational corporations as though they were sentient human beings equipped with passports and examine them in more realistic terms. But meanwhile the concept of the corporation as a citizen should not get in the way of serious analysis.

G. W. B.

The corporate citizen does business outside the country of its nationality by sufferance of the local state, which, in the language of fiction and fantasy, is the "host government." If the corporate citizen affronts the "host," it can—like a human guest—be expelled and, like an innkeeper who impounds the guest's laundry, the "host" government may confiscate whatever immovable property the guest company leaves behind by processes euphemistically

described as "nationalization," "expropriation," or—more recently
—a gradually increasing "participation."

There is no doubt that the government of a host country has the
power to tax, regulate, expropriate, and expel any company that
does business within its borders. The problems arise because it can,
as a general rule, control only that part of the company's activities
that are physically within its jurisdiction; it does not have the same
degree of effective control over the whole of the guest company's
operations that, at least in theory, it would possess were the
company a local corporate citizen, locally owned and managed.

As a matter of rough distinction, it is probably useful to separate
the complaints of the governments of less developed countries from
those of the governments of the more advanced states, since the
ability of advanced host governments to control the affairs of guest
companies is necessarily more effective.

The complaints of host governments of less developed countries
reflect a number of grievances.

One grievance arises from the fact that the managements of
multinational companies are likely to command greater resources
and be more sophisticated than the governments of poor nations
and, because such companies operate over wider geographical
areas, they have more options. Consider, for example, intracorporate pricing and costing. To a considerable extent a large integrated
company can control the amounts of money it earns in a host
country by manipulating the prices it charges the local subsidiary
for its products and the costs it allocates to it. Thus, by controlling
transfer prices the management can, within limits, determine its
own base for local taxation and even avoid exchange controls and
efforts to limit repatriation. Though the host government can insist
on seeing the books of the local subsidiary, it cannot examine the
books of the parent, and, even if it could, it would not have the
highly trained manpower to make informed reallocations of
earnings and costs.

Yet that is only one of the complaints that result from the fact
that the affairs of the guest company are controlled by an absentee
management located outside the host country which, in deploying
its resources, has, within limits, the ability to pick and choose

among tax systems and national regulations. So long as the host country has jurisdiction merely over the part of the company's activities within its borders and does not have jurisdiction over the company's principal profit center, it is frequently at a disadvantage in dealing with a corporate management that can move its resources about flexibly.

Still, the stereotype of the giant company playing fast and loose with the efforts of a host country to control it requires substantial qualification in the light of recent experience.

In every case the host country can refuse to permit a guest company to perform certain types of operations, or even to operate at all within its borders. But, in such a contest, the relative bargaining power of the two parties can no longer be taken for granted because the guest company does not always have practicable options.

We have seen this principle illustrated by the David and Goliath struggle in the Middle East, where a group of small nations have worked their will on some of the largest and most powerful multinational companies. As a result of the comparatively low cost of producing Middle Eastern oil, the existence of a world shortage, and their success in maintaining a common front, the Middle Eastern governments have been able to exact exorbitant revenues from, and impose exorbitant conditions on, the major international oil companies, to the point of compelling them to serve as political instruments for enforcing an embargo against their own domiciliary country as though their tanker fleets were part of the Arab navy.

To be sure, the situation will not often occur where small states can exact such high tribute. The basic requirement is the possession of some unique quality of soil or sub-soil that yields an essential commodity in world demand—whether mineral or agricultural—and so denies the foreign corporate citizen the option to go elsewhere.

Thus the central question—whether a poor country possesses the essential bargaining chips—depends more on the interplay of markets and resources than on any inherent limitations on the jurisdictional reach of its government. It is a question that affects a whole range of relations, not merely those between multinational corporations and national governments but between the governments of rich and poor countries. For years the less developed countries have been complaining of an alleged secular trend in the terms of trade against the interests of raw material producers, while they have insistently demanded a preferential position in the markets of the industrialized nations.

Since the test of bargaining strength against the multinational company derives from economic factors, the decisive issue is not whether the less developed country is the domicile or merely the host of the company. The bargaining strength of the multinational company depends on its mobility, and, if it can afford to abandon operations in a particular country, it can move its domicile and headquarters almost as easily as it can redeploy its other assets and activities. Efforts of national governments to respond by expropriating properties or dictating the conditions of production under systems of national planning are in either case more likely to result in the impoverishment of the country than in stimulating a great leap forward.

It would serve little purpose, therefore, to try to extend the jurisdiction of host governments to reach or influence the activities of corporations outside their borders. Nor would it be at all practicable; if each host government were to try independently to reallocate the costs and income of a guest company so as to maximize the revenues It could reach by taxes or to insist that the company locate a substantial part of its research and development activities, or conduct a high percentage of fabricating operations within its boundaries, the company could be hopelessly crippled by conflicting and contradictory pressures.

One parenthesis may be useful at this point. If some think I am expressing excessive solicitude for the multinational corporation, it is not from any ideological bias. I see no greater virtue in corporate managements than government bureaucracies—in fact, no inherent virtue in either. They are merely two forms of organizing mankind's energies that have so far survived Huxley's social Darwinism. But, just as I believe that the nation-state—at our present level of political evolution—is an indispensable institutional form, so it seems to me that the organization of economic activities through multinational companies offers values well worth preserving. Simplistic as the concept may seem to some—and that is the currently fashionable term of denigration—the multinational company does provide the best mechanism anyone has so far suggested for utilizing the world's resources efficiently.

Though I recognize that Adam Smith's reverence for the worldwide division of labor is no longer shared by those who believe it perpetuates injustices, the correction of those injustices is not likely to be achieved by action at the local level. Again, our own experience may have some relevance, for the experience of the American states to which I referred in my earlier chapter did little to correct the disparities in wealth between the rich and poorer sections of the country. That correction got under way in the recent postwar years only when industry took advantage of the mobility made possible by a vast free market to exploit certain natural advantages the South then offered—and, at roughly the same time, the federal government undertook practical programs to improve income distribution among the several states.

So far we have made only token efforts at the international level to narrow the gulf between rich and poor nations—or at least to keep it from widening more swiftly than would otherwise be the case. We have transferred resources from the public sector through the World Bank and its affiliates, some agencies of the United Nations, and a few regional development banks, but that is only scratching the surface of the problem. The day when we will make a frontal assault with sufficient scope and magnitude appears far in the future.

Meanwhile indiscriminate local interference with the operation of multinational corporations seems likely to do more harm than good. To be sure, there are many who contend that the development of the multinational corporation is more likely to encourage oligopoly than competition and that such companies do not achieve the efficiencies I have suggested. Managements, it is pointed out, may, in some cases, be influenced by considerations other than the pure profit motive—which, of course, could be partially the case. Admittedly, the multinational corporation, as I have described it for purposes of this discussion, is more archetypal than real; no serious observer would contend that the managements of most multinational companies have yet developed that refinement of thought where they consciously weave their corporate plans on the seamless web of something called the world economy. But the point is that many are moving in that direction, and, unless resurgent nationalism interrupts the process, they will approach progressively closer to that ideal.

Small poor nations cannot prevent the creation of international oligopolies by national laws, even if they regarded the creation of free competition as a good thing—which most of them manifestly do not—while interference at the local level is more likely to result in distortions and inefficient resource use than in making the poor richer. For, if multinational companies have not yet achieved the ultimate goal of operating with full efficiency within the world market, it is—in part at least—because the governments of nation-states have created rigidities and obstructions, seeking, all too often, to force the multinational companies to conform to the Procrustean limitations of small national markets. That is not a very useful endeavor. My heart is not lifted at the prospect of a map speckled with small, medium-sized, and large autarkies that would waste resources deplorably. Nor can a worldwide division of labor be achieved merely by permitting the free movement of goods unless the other factors of production are also permitted to move freely.

Charles P. Kindleberger

6

The Multinational Corporation in a World of Militant Developing Countries

For many years the relations between huge multinational companies and small nation-states were regarded as an unequal contest, since the multinational company could deploy overwhelming resources of money, mobility, and sophistication. Today, however, particularly in the case of extractive industries where the multinational company is bound to the host state by immobile investments, relative bargaining power is undergoing a rapid shift. The experience of the international oil companies—the classbook example of huge mobile international companies—with the OPEC countries has challenged old assumptions.

G. W. B.

In a penetrating study entitled *American Corporations and Peruvian Politics*, Charles T. Goodsell describes the Velasco-led government of Peru which came to power through a coup in 1968 as revolutionary.

CHARLES P. KINDLEBERGER *is Ford Professor of International Economics at M.I.T. A former division chief in the State Department's Bureau of Economic Affairs, he has written many books on international economics and foreign trade.*

> Its principal values were uncompromising nationalism and economic populism; by systematic changes throughout the society and economy, the aim was to reduce social and economic inequalities, foster economic growth, and terminate dependence on the United States.

"Uncompromising nationalism and economic populism" and the aim to "terminate dependence on the United States" or the developed world seem to me to characterize the environment in which the multinational corporation has had to operate vis-à-vis developing countries in the last decade or so.

Whether it is possible to reduce social and economic inequalities, to foster economic growth and to terminate dependence on the United States, all at the same time, poses a question of fundamental importance for developing countries. Opinion on the role of private investment in economic development of underdeveloped countries ranges widely from the views of Presidents Eisenhower and Nixon that private investment ought to be relied upon exclusively to furnish outside assistance, to those of the school which finds all investment and even foreign aid abhorrent and subversive of development. An Indian economist at Oxford University, Sanjaya Lall, has furnished a classification of opinion, with three classes which favor direct investment and three which oppose.

Spectrum of Views on Foreign Direct Investment

In favor of foreign investment are 1) the business school or how-to-do-it approach; 2) the traditional-economic, which emphasizes the contributions made by capital and technology; and 3) the neo-traditional, which recommends investment but some international surveillance to provide countervailing power. Opposed are 4) the nationalist school, which finds many harmful aspects in private investment, believes its profits to be excessive, and wants to regulate it stringently on a national, case-by-case basis, to capture its benefits without the evils; 5) the *dependencia* school with little coherent program, but fear of foreign investment; and 6) the Marxists with a clear-cut doctrine of opposition.

Lall names names. The business school approach includes Robbins and Stobaugh; the traditional-economic—Vernon (though he works partly in a business school) and me. Vernon and I are also partly in the neo-traditional camp. Opposed to foreign investment are Streeten and Lall in the national school; Sunkel and Hymer among the *dependencia* group; and Magdoff, Sweezy, Frank, Weisskopf *et al.* among the Marxists. If fear of dependence is akin to populism, as I believe, the antis, excluding the doctrinaire Marxists, emphasize nationalism and populism.

Economics and Politics of Direct Investment

There is a temptation to think of economics as favoring direct investment and politics as opposed. This is not accurate. We shall encounter below instances where economic and political analyses are in conflict, but there is a political side to the traditional economic view of our issue, and an economic aspect to the nationalist. On the first score, the antithesis may run between the international and national view. The traditional economic view would suggest that resources be invested worldwide where they can earn the highest return, to maximize world output in a Pareto-optimal sense. By Pareto-optimal is meant a state of resource allocation in which no reallocation can make anyone better off without making someone else worse off. It is an efficiency criterion but not necessarily the most equitable distribution of income and welfare in the world. To the extent that the resulting income distribution was unacceptable, it should be altered through progressive (or possibly regressive) contributions to international programs and foreign aid: use the price and market system to allocate resources, budgets including transfers to deal with income distribution. The nationalist school, on the contrary, believes that international compensatory transfers to accomplish income redistribution are illusory, that the task of a national government is to maximize national income even at the expense of the cosmopolis. A certain amount of restriction on trade, investment, technology transfers, and the like is acceptable despite distortion of resource allocation, if it adds to national income along lines technically known as the optimum tariff. In some cases they may be prepared to sacrifice some national income for other governmental objectives—economic objectives like higher employment or socio-political goals such as national cohesion. Mostly, however, they contemplate that the developing countries can be more independent and better off at the same time.

The clash between economics and politics is nowhere better illustrated than in the different forecasts made concerning the price of oil. My colleague, M. A. Adelman, who is a deep student of the economics of the world petroleum industry, and who believes that cost determines price in the long run, thought the world price of oil was likely to fall from its 1973 posted level of $2.60 in the Persian Gulf more nearly to $2.10 for buyers. The Organization of Petroleum Exporting Countries (OPEC) was trying to raise the price, but Adelman thought the long-run marginal cost of perhaps 35 cents a barrel exercised a strong downward pull. He may still be right.

Meanwhile, however, another economist, Walter Levy, took the opposing view that OPEC, which inherited the position of the world cartel of the interwar period that had broken down through competition, would succeed in preserving its unity against chiseling at the margin. Neither of them, it is probably fair to say, had any idea that the Yom Kippur war would produce an oil embargo for purely political reasons with such devastating economic effects in demonstrating to OPEC the short-run inelasticity of demand. A small shut-in in production, plus a scramble for inventory, resulted in a 350 percent price increase. By the same token, however, it is likely that once the tension of the Mid-East struggle is faded in memory, inching up of output by one country and another, along with small permanent reductions in demand, will make the price structure more and more difficult for OPEC to hold. Sheikh Yamani of Saudi Arabia evidently had this possibility in mind when he suggested positive price reductions in 1974. We will then be back to the 1973 position, when it was possible for the economist to predict on the basis of long-run cost that the price was too high, despite the brilliant device of an excise tax disguised as an income tax, and another to maintain that militancy of producing countries would dominate politically the economic factor of cost.

It is ironic, but not without poetic justice, that the countries

which so long complained about monopoly profits on the part of
international companies should now seek not to break up the
monopolies so much as to take them over. The position is of course
symmetrical. At the time when developed countries controlled the
monopolies, there were few voices among them which inveighed
against monopolies in foreign trade. Opposed to the Sherman and
Clayton Acts for home consumption was the Webb-Pomerene Act
which encouraged collusion in restraint of trade against foreigners.

Quasi-rents in Efficiency and Income Distribution

Much of the difficulty derives from the existence of rents and
the struggle to possess them. In a world of perfect competition and
no scarce resources, there are no rents. Price equals marginal cost
equals marginal utility in consumption. Large consumer surpluses
may exist, and some producer surpluses, if some resources are better
for the production of given outputs than others. These latter rents
are desirable in the economic system, though they create a political
problem of unequal income distribution. Recent interpretation of
the enclosures in England runs to the effect that whatever their
effect on income distribution, they were desirable in the interest of
efficiency. Without private ownership, more efficient resources will
be overused. Labor will crowd on to the best land until it drives the
average return down to the wage level; for efficiency the marginal
return of the last increment of labor should equal the wage.
Without rent, there is overcrowding, underemployment, and opportunities to increase real output by charging rent and diverting labor
into other occupations. The position can be illustrated by a problem
in today's world. In the oceans, where it is impossible to charge
rent, the better fishing grounds are overfished. Too many whales,
for example, are killed through lack of rent. If the seas could be
owned and rented, excessive resources devoted to fishing would
be shifted into other occupations and world real income would be
raised.

For efficient use of all natural resources, therefore, we need to
charge rents on the best resources, and to equalize marginal returns
on other factors on these and no-rent mines, oil wells, and land. But

in this, as in the enclosures, there is an economico-political problem as to who collects the rents. The Marxist view of the enclosures as primitive accumulation is that predatory members of society used force to push peasants off the land. There is some truth in this view, but much land was enclosed through voluntary negotiations, later ratified by Parliament. Similarly in the international economy, access to the best natural resources was sometimes arrived at on a voluntary basis and sometimes had large elements of compulsion and force. The history of imperialism in such areas as the Belgian Congo or South Africa has been a struggle for rents. Laws worked out, not without trauma, in developed societies, were applied with the help of colonial rule to the world beyond Europe. Where the natives were not eliminated, they were typically pushed aside. Even political independence, for example, from Spain in South America, did little to alter arrangements already made with respect to rents, or rules governing their future allocation. Developed countries felt that rents in resources in the developing world should go to their discoverers, or to those who developed the technology for using them effectively. Native populations when they awoke at last to the existence of such rents, and especially after World War II when political independence spread widely in the Third World, insisted that these rents belonged to the new nation.

Each group based its contention on a different counterfactual argument, that is, a different scenario, if the term be permitted, as to what would have happened if the foreign company or multinational corporation had not developed the resource. To the multinational corporation, the alternative was no development; to the newly independent country, the alternative was equivalent development, perhaps somewhat delayed, with local citizens producing the capital, technology, management, and marketing, and reaping the rents.

This last is a nationalist view, and it underlies United Nations preoccupation from 1958[1] to 1974[2] with resolutions proclaiming the

---

[1] U.N. Resolution 1314 (XIII) of 1958 established a Permanent Sovereignty Commission which proposed a Resolution of Permanent Sovereignty over National Resources 1803 (XVII) in 1962.

[2] See United Nations, Economic and Social Council E/5500/Add. 1 (Part I) "The Impact

permanent sovereignty of nation-states over the natural resources within their borders. It is perhaps ironic that the United Nations, established in the interests of internationalism, should be the vehicle of these strong expressions of nationalism.

With entry possible, and not too wide differences in the productivity of incremental resources, one would have expected competition to disperse most of the rent as consumers' surplus. This process has met resistance, however, from several sources: from owners of older resources, now rendered inefficient. Texas oil producers, and Ruhr, Durham, and Pas-de-Calais coal interests want to hold energy prices high to preserve and extend old rents. Moreover, governments in consuming countries wanted revenue as well as to protect their fuel-producers. The result has been that despite new entry—the international oil companies rising from a handful in 1928 to five, seven, and then forty by 1968—the price remained relatively high, and the rents on Saudi and Kuwaiti production intact. But competition was spreading: discoveries occurred in Libya, Nigeria, Indonesia, the gasfields off the Dutch coast, the British North Sea, and the North Slope of Alaska. New entrants lowered the price to establish a market after which they were prepared to join the cartel and shut the door. The burden of making room for them on the original five or seven international companies increased. The price started to fall.

A Digression on Exploitation

Before I recite more of the potted history of international oil, it may be well to pause briefly on a semantic point, and discuss the meaning of the words *exploitation* and *excessive profits*, which feature prominently in the debate. By exploitation I mean more than "to use" as when one exploits a given resource; in the discussion of private investment in developing countries, exploitation has a

of Multinational Corporations on the Development Process and on International Relations, Report of the Group of Eminent Persons to Study the Role of Multinational Corporations on Development and on International Relations," May 24, 1974, Section IV "Ownership and Control," and Economic and Social Council Resolution 1747 (LIV) "Permanent Sovereignty over Natural Resources of Developing Countries," adopted 4 May 1973.

pejorative connotation, closer to "abuse," or "use in some unfair fashion." It is true that one commentator who fits into the sixth category of Lall's taxonomy of views on the subject, Johann Galtung, defines dependence of any kind as "exploitation." A wife who depends on her husband is exploited, as is a husband who depends on his wife. Interdependence is mutual exploitation. *Dependencia* in category five, however, is one-sided, not mutual as in trade among developed countries, or two-way investment among the United States, Europe, and Japan. Some years ago, Edith Penrose defined exploitation by an international company as a higher price on goods sold, or a higher profit, than the minimum it would take to stay in business, *i.e.* the reserve price, or the normal rate of profit below which it would in the long-run move into another business. Where there are big rents, however, and the problem is how to divide them, all solutions are exploitive in this sense. At the country's reserve price, the country is exploiting the company. In between, each is exploiting the other. By the same token, excessive profits are any above the long-run normal rate achieved through competition, that is, rents are excess profits. In a resolution of 1968, OPEC decided that

> notwithstanding any guarantee of fiscal stability that may have been granted the operator, the operator shall not have the right to obtain excessively high net earnings after taxes. The financial provisions of contracts which actually result in such excessively high net earnings shall be open to renegotiation.[3]

Contract Renegotiation

Renegotiation of contracts is of course not unknown in developed-country jurisprudence. In defense contracts, the Pentagon used to set prices tentatively, and provide for renegotiation so that if these resulted in substantial profits based on cheaper costs than initially foreseen, prices and profits could be adjusted. A television or sport star who makes a big success suddenly is apt to have his old contract torn up and a new one written. But OPEC has

[3] Resolution XVI 90 of 1968.

made a fine point of renegotiation, based on any number of circumstances. When the dollar was devalued in December 1971, and again in February 1973, old contracts with time to run were unilaterally cancelled and new ones negotiated. Although the contracts were written in dollars, it was intolerable to OPEC to lower the price of oil in Deutschemarks, Swiss francs, or yen. Moreover, it is easy to guess that countries like France, England, and Japan which made contracts to buy oil from Iran at high prices in the winter and spring of 1974 will not be granted the same freedom to renegotiate when underlying circumstances have changed and the price of oil declines from its high level of that period.

When the economic system is working satisfactorily, high profits, or perhaps they should be called excessive profits, are a signal that a particular good is in scarce supply. Potential competitors are thereby encouraged to effect entry into the industry, stepping up their exploration efforts in oil as in the 1950s and 1960s. High profits recorded by General Motors-Holden Proprietary Co. Ltd. in Australia in the early 1950s, sharply criticized at the time, were competed away by new entry from other automotive companies from the United States, Europe, and Japan, to the evident benefit of the consumer. Entry may be impossible on a substantial scale. It may be impossible to find new strikes of the size and quality of those in Saudi Arabia and Kuwait. In these cases, high profits (rents) will persist, and will be struggled over by company and country. The company hopes for a bidding up of the value of its shares, reducing the rate of return to stockholders to a normal level; it also hopes for new and more favorable contractual arrangements when an opportunity for increased investment presents itself, and it is in position to threaten to withhold its necessary cooperation.

The country, on the other hand, raises taxes, taking over the rent in the same fashion that Henry George once proposed for the rent of land in urban settings. The country may also demand a portion of the equity of the company—25 percent, 51 percent, or the totality. In this circumstance, the rent is divided between company and country depending on the price of compensation for the part of the company sold. If the price is book value, dropping any fine points, the rents accrue to the country; if the market value at normal rates of taxation, to the company. These do not represent the limits, of course. In the IPC case in Peru, the country entered a claim for back taxes on long distributed or reinvested profits, which wiped out the company equity. And a usual tactic is to offer to pay book value not in a single sum but over an extended period and without interest, which renders its present discounted value well below book.

The initial deal may have involved duress (a gunboat in the harbor), unequal bargaining power (between, say, tough Dutchmen and the Indians who sold Manhattan for $24 worth of beads and other trade goods), misrepresentation, extraterritoriality, bribery, corruption, lack of disclosure and any one or more of a long list of faults which would invalidate a modern contract. Or they may not. In *American Corporations and Peruvian Politics* Goodsell finds that the *dependencia* and Marxist view, that American corporations control domestic politics by bribes, favors, domination of the mass media, and intervention by the American government to establish economic dependence of Peru on the companies, is sustained in part but refuted in part. Similarly the alternative "business-school" hypothesis that American corporations avoid participation, minimize visibility, and bargain effectively over investment terms is verified to some extent but not totally. The most scandalous episodes recounted by Goodsell for Peru, and by Barnet and Müller in a new populist American account of the MNC, *Global Reach*, have a musty flavor and go back to the 1920s. There are an occasional ITT Chile episode and plausible allegations such as those about the CIA in Iraq in 1950 and Guatemala in 1954. Goodsell makes the persuasive case, however, that a wide variety of conduct exists on the part of American corporations, and that once the Peruvian Junta nationalized IPC, the Grace properties, the Morrison-Knudsen property, and after General Motors quit the country the "revolutionary" government first ignored the remaining corporations, and then quietly began dialogue with them to induce new investments and to make existing ones more productive.

In economics, by-gones are by-gones, sunk costs to be forgotten. Historical wrongs, however, have a present discounted value for politicians who can win short-term victories with them. Once the politicians have gained power—which earns a rent for them—their objective function is likely to change. The economic gain from prospective development becomes more important than the political benefit of beating a dead horse, and nationalism, populism, and *dependencia* as slogans become blocks to getting business done. An insecure government like Amin's in Uganda, Allende's in Chile, and even Frei's in Chile needs to nationalize another foreign corporation each six months. Once secure, it may be necessary to disguise the fact of paying compensation for past appropriations, by converting the capital sum due into a management fee on a marketing contract. It was alleged in the press, although I have lost the reference, that Peru nationalized the Chase Manhattan Bank branch with an excessive level of compensation, to assuage the Rockefeller owners of both Chase Manhattan and IPC for the derisory compensation for the latter—although the story makes little sense on its face given the disparity in the ownership of the two institutions. But the political benefits of nationalistic gestures, and the subsequent costs of appearing to undo them may require a certain degree of political dissembling to cover economic cooperation.

Transfer Pricing

In one important respect, a "wrong" is current rather than historic. Some years ago, Australia found that ostensibly competing oil companies had very different profits. One, a joint venture owned 50-50 by Australian and American interests, earned respectable profits in Australia and paid Australian corporate income taxes. Others, 100 percent foreign-owned, earned no profits in Australia and paid no income tax. Their profits were earned in the Middle East where they qualified for depletion allowances and lower taxes. Vertically-integrated oil companies, where there was no need to keep local shareholders happy, tended to arrange transfer prices between stages so as to reap their profits at the crude-oil level where taxes were least. Later, a Harvard Development Advisory Service representative discovered that some pharmaceutical companies were earning no profits and paying no taxes in Colombia, and paying prices on purchase of intermediate products from a Panama subsidiary, which accumulated the profits of the company in a tax shelter there.

Evidence on transfer pricing is difficult to obtain, of course, and most tax authorities are not as astute as was Constantine Vaitsos, the adviser in question. It is accordingly difficult to know how widespread the practice is. True believers from either the business-school approach or from the *dependencia*-Marxist school will tend to hold different views on the same limited amount of evidence. In the United States, a businessman informs me, a ruling by the Internal Revenue Service that transfer prices would be policed to see that they conformed to the arm's length, competitive price, or a simulated facsimile thereof, turned virtually every American company into a model taxpayer in this respect overnight. This may or may not be so. In the underdeveloped world of the nationalist, *dependencia* or Marxist school, pharmaceutical transfer-pricing lives on in generalized form. Siphoning off the rent through transfer pricing may or may not take place, but is suspected everywhere.

The tension between the economic and the political views of the multinational corporation is nowhere better illustrated, as a crucial experiment for the next months, than in the debate over whether the crunch in oil will be followed by similar squeezes in other primary products. Already in motion is a series of efforts to raise taxes on bananas, bauxite, copper, tin, and the like. If the OPEC success is purely political, it is likely to be followed by others, as C. Fred Bergsten has predicted in *Foreign Policy*. If, on the other hand militancy is not enough, and the elasticities must be low, these efforts will not succeed. Consumption of bananas will decline relative to apples, grapefruit, oranges, etc., and aluminum use will decline relative to steel.

Fighting over rents is perhaps the main issue in the tension between the MNC and the less developed country (LDC). There is, however, another profound issue—the extent to which economic development should and can use market signals. The MNC responds to the market, even where it does not manipulate it. If the LDC is convinced that resources should not be allocated according to market signals, it will and should resist the MNC. Where the market does not work, even the traditional economist does not insist on using it. In economic jargon, with market failure we are in the realm of the second best. And the only valid argument for tariffs, or against direct investment, is the second best. Something is wrong with the market which gives off misleading signals. In this case it is a mistake to follow its prescription.

Market Efficiency in LDCs

Markets do not work when there is monopoly, imperfect information, failure of households, factors, or firms to respond to price signals. In these circumstances prices reflect neither scarcities nor needs, or to the extent that they do, they fail to elicit the appropriate response. For one example, take the infant-industry argument for a tariff or against foreign investment. With perfect information and perfect capital markets, local entrepreneurs would not need a tariff—or restrictions on foreign investors. They would be able to borrow to cover early losses or less-than-normal profits. Or take the Colombian pharmaceutical case: the first-best solution is to watch import prices and enforce the rule of arms-length prices in intracompany dealings. Only if this is impossible, is it valid as second-best to exclude foreign investors because of potential exploitation.

A general case can be made by the nationalists, *dependencia* school, and Marxists that the market in developing countries does not and will not represent social priorities. Consumer sovereignty is barred because of the alleged distortions of advertising, excessive product differentiation, and consumer ignorance. Foreign firms should not be allowed to borrow in the capital market which is underdeveloped, which needs to learn by doing, and which might be stunted in its development were it to be monopolized by foreign borrowers. Foreign firms bring in the wrong technology, responding to factor proportions in the home country and the benefits of standardization. The best is the enemy of the good. The second or third best may be good enough, or as good as one can hope for. Included in the second or third best may be wide-ranging control of foreign enterprise.

Or so the argument runs, though it is seldom so explicitly made. Nor is it always consistent with another argument that intervention in the market by developing countries is so fraught with mistakes that they must be prevented, for example, from bidding for foreign investment by an Andes pact which limits national sovereignty and the right to intervene separately.

There is something of a contradiction between seeking to appropriate the rents which are provided by the market, and rejecting the market altogether as a guide to what to produce, how to produce it, and for whom. Manipulation and rejection are not perhaps entirely orthogonal, but they are close to it. And those who reject the market have the task of deciding what to use in its stead. Even traditional economics is prepared to recognize that the market does not provide divine revelation of the directions in which the economy, polity, and society should move. For all its failures, however, it tends to be like democracy—better than the attainable alternatives. Populism makes a strong case against the capital, credit, money, primary-product, consumers-goods, capital-goods, and labor market. Dispensing altogether with markets and substituting planning with quantities rather than prices, or interfering in markets based on bureaucratic or politician intuition are likely to be worse.

There is little likelihood of closing the gap between the pros and the cons. The position is brilliantly illustrated by the United Nations report of the Group of Eminent Persons, and especially by Part II, the "Comments of Individual Members." Since the report of Eminent Persons had a faint nationalist and populist bias, though less than the staff report *Multinational Corporations in World Development*, five of the nine individual comments (out of twenty members) came from developed countries: two from the United States and one each from Japan, Sweden, and Switzerland, and all were long, detailed, and traditional-economic. The comments from the Algerian, Chilean, Indian, and Yugoslav members were short and nationalist or Marxist, but in one instance recommended the incorporation in the report of Eminent Persons of the staff report.

Where there is no meeting of minds, it seems to me useless to paper the cracks. I believe in an international body to deal with problems arising in connection with multinational corporations among the developed countries, with a broadly similar point of view. Between the developed and the developing countries, however, it seems premature. Where there is no meeting of minds, agreement on a form of words, and the creation of machinery for discussion, are idle. Let the market decide. I suggest that the Eminent Persons recommendation of a commission to run a watching brief on the multinational corporation is likely merely to institutionalize the nationalism and populism of the developing countries. On previous occasions I have urged that governments of developed countries withdraw from this field, cancelling their investment subsidies, guarantees, and tax credits. Companies can then decide on economic grounds, with allowance for political risk, whether it is worthwhile to invest in developing countries, and developing countries, in their turn, can decide whether and on what terms they want foreign investment. If the dependence is mutual, as I believe, this market will be able to strike a bargain.

Herbert Salzman

7

How to Reduce and Manage
the Political Risks of Investment
in Less Developed Countries

In view of the new militancy of host countries, managements of multinational enterprises need to sharpen their political skills and devise careful strategies for minimizing the risks of doing business, particularly in the less developed countries.

G. W. B.

Economic nationalism has been an increasing threat to United States foreign direct investment in recent years, particularly to large extractive or natural resource-related enterprises. United States firms have been involved in investment disputes with host governments on an increasing scale and in a manner that poses difficult economic and foreign policy questions for the United States government and presents severe problems to existing and prospective United States foreign investors.

Traditional responses to the new issues involved have not been

HERBERT SALZMAN *is a director of the Overseas Private Investment Corporation. In 1966–71 he was in the Office of Private Resources, Agency for International Development. Before entering government service, Mr. Salzman had a distinguished business career as president of the Standard Bag Corporation.*

adequate. The United States government and certain private investors have devised some ingenious, pragmatic measures that tend to reduce the risk and mitigate the damage caused by nationalization. These measures are based on several premises.

First, it is recognized that there is no legally enforceable way to bind a sovereign state that does not voluntarily wish to be so bound. In investment disputes, a sovereign state will tend to use its economic and political areas of comparative advantage to further what it perceives to be its own domestic and foreign interests.

Second, it is possible for the parent country, the host country, and private investors, as parties to the investment, to balance their interests, and desirable that they optimize their benefits over the longer term based on informed self-interest. However, changing circumstances will change the relative strengths of the parties and affect their relations.

Third, an orderly way of effecting the necessary adjustments in sharing of costs and benefits is preferable to the alternative of confrontation, conflict, and resolution by force. Time often enables people and institutions to make tolerable adjustments to change and enough time must, therefore, be a vital element in resolving disputes.

Finally, international consensus is the ultimate determinant of merit and legitimacy in investment disputes. United States government short-term efforts should be conducted so as to enhance its longer-term credibility and the validity of its position in the international forums of the world community.

An increasing number of governments, particularly in Latin America, have challenged both the existence of international law requiring prompt and adequate compensation and the right of a foreign government or international body to intervene in any way to assert or enforce such a law in their sovereign realms. The withholding of aid, whether bilateral or multilateral, is of little significance to many governments. The United States also is frequently reluctant to jeopardize other interests—military, political, and the continuance of other American investment in the country—by precipitating a confrontation with a government that has mistreated a U.S. investor.

Protection of U.S. foreign investors is becoming increasingly important as foreign investment takes a place with trade and monetary policies as the major components of U.S. foreign economic policy. In the absence of any binding international agreements, the transnational investor must continue to reduce his risks via the mechanisms described below, and the U.S. government must improve its instruments for the protection of American foreign investment. Measures so far developed to prevent and reduce risks may become elements of an emerging system that can successfully cope with international economic issues transcending national boundaries.

Factors in Investment Disputes

Most countries, including the United States and many LDCs, are involved in a major redistribution of their national resources and drastic changes in their international economic relations. In some instances, the changes might lead to a fundamental transformation of the society. Inflation, high food and fuel costs, high unemployment, and concerns about national independence and dependence—common issues capable of arousing the public worldwide—have long been familiar in the LDCs.

The causes of economic nationalism are complex. Many citizens of poorer countries believe they have not derived benefits proportionate to those of the foreign investor or his parent country. Many resent their poverty and dependence on foreign companies and blame the foreigners' international economic power for both. Such beliefs and resentments, when coupled with rising expectations, may exert inexorable political pressures for immediate action, without regard for possible future adverse economic consequences, and in some instances even increase its income, *e.g.,* the Organization of Petroleum Exporting Countries (OPEC).

Economic nationalism is one form of political response. Whether or not it results in an increase in productivity or access to larger markets, economic nationalism can often help a government—beleaguered from political and budgetary pressure—maintain and even increase its domestic popularity. The domestic benefits of action may thus appear far greater than the possible costs.

The large, visible enterprise is the natural target for nationalization, particularly if it is foreign owned. Yet, while sovereign states may expropriate foreign property, international law requires fair compensation. Since that is subject to varied interpretation, the determination of the value of the expropriated property is the core issue for negotiation.

The U.S. Treasury must involuntarily share the book value losses sustained by an American investor as a result of uncompensated expropriation, because such losses are deductible for tax purposes. Though the opportunity costs are not deductible, the Treasury still loses the taxes it would otherwise receive on the future earnings of the company. The result is that our government participates in investors' losses on a non-selective basis and with no opportunity to exercise its judgment regarding the "fairness" of the appropriation regardless of its very real financial interest.

As a target for nationalization, the transnational company (TNC) does not correspond to the popular image of the foreign entrepreneur intent on squeezing profits from colonial or neo-colonial areas. Historically, the foreign investment has been privately owned, whereas the ownership of the modern TNC ranges from wholly private to wholly government owned. The TNC serves a global market, and is therefore primarily concerned with the economics of worldwide production and distribution. However, its very size makes it a vital factor in the policies of the host countries.

Economic nationalism is not limited to LDCs. Canadianization is a comparatively recent manifestation of resentment of heavy U.S. investment in Canada. The "American Challenge" caused intense reactions in Europe to the growing U.S. investment there. The Japanese, until recently, banned significant foreign direct investment in Japan and still strictly regulate its inflow. Finally, the recent Japanese and Arab direct investment in the United States caused a stir here, even though the United States itself is the world's largest foreign direct investor.

Moreover, economic nationalism is not exclusively aimed at foreign investors. Governments frequently nationalize domestic properties in pursuit of state control. In practice, this means that foreign investors are likely to suffer most if they control a principal enterprise in a key sector of an LDC economy. For example, in India, shipping, airlines, life insurance, and general insurance companies have been nationalized, and Zambia has taken over key mining, industrial, and transportation enterprises. Pakistan has subjected to government control 31 firms in the 10 industry categories considered essential to the national interest.

The LDC government and the large enterprise are the principal, but not the sole, parties involved in investment disputes. Others with an important stake in the outcome include: the parent country government; competitors in the same industry; other foreign investors in other industries in the same country; customers who depend on the enterprise as a source of supply; commercial banks with loans outstanding; development lending and other international financial institutions such as the United States Agency for International Development (AID), Inter-American Development Bank (IDB), the World Bank (IBRD), and the International Monetary Fund (IMF); and export bankers, such as The Export-Import Bank, and other export credit banks. Each is concerned primarily with its own special responsibilities, and their views may be expected to vary accordingly.

One major issue in investment disputes is the determination of "fair" valuation of expropriated property. On the one hand, transnational companies generally believe "adequate" compensation should be based on "going concern" value. They consider historic costs and profits a guide to future profits and expect that valuation to take these into account. On the other hand, LDC governments tend to base the valuation on historic costs, *i.e.*, book value or, perhaps, updated book value.

Settlements have tended to be based on book value, and thus compensation settlements have in practice differed substantially from the compensation norm defined by the U.S. government as "prompt, adequate and effective."

In some cases, LDCs deemed book value to be "adequate"; in others, deductions were taken to cover alleged overpriced construction costs, or insufficient reserves for depreciation. "Prompt" has sometimes meant payment in low-interest bearing, nonmarketable long-term bonds. "Effective" in some instances meant nonconvertible local currency, or perhaps a requirement to reinvest the proceeds in the LDC. A major factor in determining compensation can be the retroactive effect of host government decisions. In the case of International Petroleum Company, Peru assessed retroactive taxes on previous earnings considered to have been excessive. In India, nationalization has not been retroactive, but as each new investment license or contract came up for expansion or renewal, new terms were negotiated.

Numerous nonlegal factors affect the negotiating strengths that determine compensation amounts, including the nature of and age of the investment, previous history, ownership, and type of product. Export market and foreign exchange earnings and domestic political partisanship may also have a bearing on the negotiations. Other aspects of the relations between the host and parent countries, including their relative power, their relations with third countries and international financial institutions, and any treaties or agreements between the governments, may have a decisive influence. Finally, the interest of the host country in attracting other new investment occasionally carries some weight.

Important changes have taken place in the type of investment disputes involving U.S. foreign investors. The 1974 State Department study reported that 71 percent of the disputes initiated before July 1, 1971 involved formal expropriation or nationalization as compared to only 22 percent in the following two-year period. In the latter period almost 80 percent of the disputes involved government coercion on U.S. investors and any foreign partners to divest themselves of all or part of their holdings or to renegotiate the terms of the investment to provide the government with a greater share of the earnings. Among the coercive tactics used have been discriminatory taxation, withholding of licenses, blocking of price increases, and bureaucratic delays.

Governments may also exert collective pressure as in the case of the Organization of Petroleum Exporting Countries (OPEC), or as is being done and attempted in the International Bauxite Association (IBA) and in the Inter-governmental Council of Copper-Exporting Countries (CIPEC). Concerted action may develop in agricultural commodities too, such as the Organization of Banana-Exporting Countries and the Association of Natural Rubber-Producing Countries.

Four advantages for the host country underlie the growing popularity of increasing participation as opposed to formal expropriation. The enterprise involved is denied a *prima facie* claim to compensation under international law; settlement terms have generally been more favorable to the host country government; widespread unfavorable publicity may be avoided; and the government may gain greater tactical negotiating flexibility.

The lower-key administrative measures to compel sale or renegotiation have so far been successful. The government has usually obtained the degree of participation or increased revenues it sought although at a cost of possible reduced attractiveness to other future private investments. Thus coerced sales or renegotiations of investment terms will continue to be the favored form of investment dispute, and investors would be well-advised to prepare themselves accordingly.

As the form of investment disputes was changing, the number of investment disputes involving U.S. foreign direct investors rose sharply. The 1974 State Department Study showed a 24 percent increase compared to the preceding two years. The book value of the property in the 89 disputes that occurred in 1971–1973 was estimated to be at least $1.5 billion. The aggregate book value of the 143 investments involved in disputes in July 1973 may run as high as $3.5 billion. This compares with estimates of past expropriations in Mainland China (1946–49) of $41 million, Eastern Europe (1946–49) of $282 million, and in Cuba (1959–60) of $956 million. Such estimates are only crude indications of the values involved. Valuations of capital assets vary widely as does the ratio to be applied to capitalization of earnings reductions that have been "renegotiated." For example, present estimates of the net increase of the Organization of Petroleum Exporting Countries (OPEC) oil revenues vary from $45 to $80 billion per year.

Of the 143 investment disputes in 39 foreign countries 59 percent (84) were in Latin America, 23 percent in Africa, and the balance in Asia. The number of disputes in Latin America is roughly proportional to the size of United States investment in the region in relation to its investment in other developing areas. Of the 84 Latin American cases, 38 were in Chile.

Over 55 percent of the 143 cases were takeovers of resource or resource-related investments, the majority of which were in oil investments. The remaining 45 percent involved banking and insurance (15 percent), and public utilities (6 percent), with the rest spread among chemicals, large land holdings, and manufacturing and distribution facilities.

Foreign investment is important to the U.S. domestic economy. Besides supplying strategic raw materials or other products that the United States needs, LDCs represent a large potential market for U.S. capital and services. As the United States continues to become more of a service economy, our interest in global markets will continue to increase. Sales in 1973 from U.S. foreign investments are estimated at about $200 billion.

The U.S. foreign investment at stake is sizable. 1973 preliminary estimates indicated a worldwide direct investment value of $102 billion (up $7 billion over 1972), of which 27 percent is in LDCs and 18 percent in Latin America. The 1973 increase in LDCs was $2.7 billion: 60 percent was in Latin America, 18 percent in Asia, 23 percent in the Middle East, and no increase in Africa. One-half of the increase was net U.S. capital outflow, and the balance represented retained earnings and Eurodollar loans.

Government Protection of Foreign Investors

Historically, the United States, along with other Western countries, has accepted the responsibility to protect its citizens and their rights abroad. Since World War II, other factors have contributed to the willingness of industrialized countries to back up their foreign investors. Private foreign investments were seen as natural complements to massive governmental aid programs and were sometimes thought to be essential to procure strategic raw materials for the United States. Capital and know-how were often invested in LDCs to provide new sources of cheaper labor-intensive products that could no longer be competitively produced in the United States. Finally, foreign investment was viewed as another means of U.S. access to a global market of huge potential.

Since the early 1960s, when all private foreign direct investment was viewed as contributing to economic development in the LDCs, the U.S. Congress has moved to modify this concept. The idea of selectivity was adopted in 1969 when the Foreign Assistance Act established criteria for specific private investments to qualify for U.S. government investment incentives.

By 1973, some in the Congress felt that the foreign investment interests of U.S. firms might differ substantially from U.S. government interests. The report of the Senate Foreign Relations Sub-Committee on Multinational Corporations said, "It [Congress] is no longer prepared to embrace the alternative theory that foreign investment, in and of itself, is a 'good thing.' " In the wake of the ITT-Chile disclosures, the Sub-Committee wished to avoid government involvement in disputes of foreign investors with host governments and opposed federal insurance of U.S. private investment because it "tends to increase the likelihood of U.S. government involvement in the internal policies of other countries in connection with the property interests of U.S. corporations."

On the other hand, that same year the House Foreign Affairs Sub-Committee on Foreign Economic Policy supported U.S. government investment incentives because "Private investment which is responsive to the economic attitudes and plans of a developing country can serve to assist that country's economic and social development. In return, some direct economic benefits, such as increased trade opportunities, will accrue to the United States." The Sub-Committee found that the Overseas Private Investment Corporation (OPIC) could play an important role in influencing the quality, form, and behavior of U.S. foreign investments and strongly emphasized OPIC "potential for minimizing intergovernmental confrontations." The Sub-Committee recommended that because of OPIC expertise in handling investment disputes, it should, by Executive Order, "be made an obligatory participant in governmental responses to any requests by a U.S.-based investor, whether insured or not, for assistance in or espousal of any claim of impairment of the investor's rights against a foreign government."

In 1972 the President of the United States issued a policy statement on investment protection in the wake of the nationalization of U.S. private enterprises, particularly in Latin America, in the hope of inhibiting similar attempts in other countries. The policy statement included the following:

> The United States has a right to expect that any taking of American private property will be non-discriminatory; for the public purpose; and that its citizens will receive prompt, adequate and effective compensation from the expropriating country.
>
> Otherwise, . . . the U.S. will not extend new bilateral economic benefits to the expropriating country . . . unless there are major factors affecting U.S. interests. . . .
>
> . . . The United States Government will withhold its support from loans under consideration in multilateral development banks.

Traditionally the intercession of the U.S. government to protect an overseas investor has been the responsibility of the State Department, which proceeds on a case-by-case basis. The Department's area of discretion has been wide, the guidelines few, and the means to evaluate the dispute limited.

Ordinarily, the investor is first required to exhaust his remedies in the local courts. This requirement may be waived if it is decided that there are no local courts that have jurisdiction, that pursuit of legal remedies in the local courts will be futile, or that the issue is of critical importance to the United States.

Should the U.S. government decide to intercede, usually its first step will be an offer to lend its "good offices" in the resolution of the dispute while at the same time expressing its concern to the host country government. "Good offices," which may be formal or informal, private or public, but are generally informal and private, are intended to facilitate negotiations and may go as far as substantial mediation. If the dispute does not yield to "good offices" and the arguments of the investor are found to have merit, the U.S. government may formally make a diplomatic claim upon the host country. There is no international forum to which the United States may appeal such claims since the U.S. law, like that of many other countries, does not permit referral of U.S. government legal matters to the World Court, except by specific acquiescence of both country parties to the dispute—an exceedingly rare occurrence in expropriation claims. Unresolved investor claims are registered by the State Department as provided under the International Claims Settlement Act of 1949, as amended. If settlement is ultimately worked out, a pro-rata distribution of the proceeds is made to the registered claimants. In March 1973, for example, an agreement was reached with Hungary in settlement of compensation claims resulting from post-World War II expropriation. The settlement is expected to be about forty cents on the dollar of the principal amount of the investment, with no interest payable for the intervening period.

Traditional diplomatic intercession has two shortcomings. First, it ignores the importance of assessing in advance the merits of the proposed investment from the U.S. government point of view. Early involvement should clarify the U.S. government's subsequent position and allow selective protection should a dispute later arise. Second, if the diplomatic process does succeed, it is unlikely to do so in time to help the specific investor. This poses a dilemma because the traditional means of dispute settlement no longer appear to work without the threat of force traditionally used to back them up.

The State Department view has been that it seldom serves U.S. government interests to become actively involved in investment disputes unless a confrontation threatens overall U.S. interests. The U.S. government's ability to protect U.S. investment in disputes is thought to be ineffective in some cases, influential in others, and decisive in only a few. The State Department recognizes reluctantly, however, that the U.S. government is apt to be ultimately drawn into an unresolved dispute of any significance because the law requires aid cut-offs.

International financial institutions have also been unable to provide effective investment protection. The World Bank (IBRD) is reluctant to become involved although its published policy is that it must deal with compensation disputes and repudiation or default on contractual agreements "substantially affecting [the host country's] international credit standing." It further says that "The Bank seeks to promote prompt and adequate settlements. . . . It initially tries to avoid passing on the merits of the dispute and to limit its role to improving communications between parties and impressing them with the desirability of a settlement."

The World Bank could take at least two constructive steps to ameliorate the settlement process for investment disputes without necessarily compromising its role as a development institution. First, in specific instances of significant investment disputes, the Bank could appoint, as a friend of the court, a panel of impartial and well regarded people not nationals of any countries involved in the dispute to establish the facts of the case. They would not judge the merits of the case but establish and publicize its factual history, using accounting audits, engineering surveys, lawyers and other skilled professionals as needed. Second, an International Investment Insurance Agency (IIIA) has long been proposed as an integral part of the World Bank system to issue political risk insurance of foreign investment against expropriation, war and convertibility. Like national insurance programs, it would selectively encourage individual private investments deemed to contribute to development, assist the settlement of investment disputes when they arise, and mitigate the effect of damages.

While an international code of conduct to govern relations between host governments and foreign private investors has the appeal associated with any abstract ideal, to be effective it must engage all the parties involved—the host government, the local enterprise, the foreign investor in that enterprise, and the foreign investor's home government. There is no mandatory legal forum with the power to enforce such "codes of conduct" if established; their purpose is to influence thinking by governments and businessmen.

A further question is whether the private investor can turn to foreign courts for legal remedies. For example, as of April, 1973, Kennecott had instituted court proceedings in five separate European countries to enforce its remedies for the recovery of part of its property, or the proceeds, on the grounds that its property in Chile had been confiscated without the compensation provided in international law. In 1972, a French court "expressly reaffirmed that no legal effect is given in France to an expropriation by a foreign state without an equitable indemnity" and that "a valid claim exists in favor of Kennecott." In 1973, the Chilean Copper Company appealed the denial of its plea that as an entity of a sovereign state, its actions were outside the jurisdiction of foreign courts. Also in 1973, a German court said that "Chile's expropriation without adequate compensation . . . violated international law and German public policy and both are entirely unbearable under the court's view of legality and morality."

At this writing the effectiveness of these judgments remains to be seen and further court action was suspended pending the outcome of negotiations between Kennecott and the government of Chile.

Risk Reduction Measures

Given the unsatisfactory mechanisms for the resolution of international investment disputes, it is important to take steps to reduce the probability that such disputes will occur. Today the TNC strategy must be to attempt to optimize profits over the long term while attempting to insure that a nationalization would not cripple the entire company.

The TNC needs to make a careful precommitment project analysis to lessen the possibility of a dispute and to determine how both the LDC and U.S. governments see their own interests. A selective investment policy at the beginning is the first, best step in the protection of the private direct foreign investment. Such an analysis must include a detailed study of the economy of the host country and the specific conditions relating to the direct investment. Moreover, a careful analysis of the financial structure of the project and dispute settlement procedures may prevent future disputes and ease the settlement of any that may arise. Following are some examples of steps that can be taken in the investment process to lessen the risk of future conflict with the host country. The illustrations are taken from natural resource related investments, which are most subject to disputes.

First, there is less likelihood of future pressures to expropriate if the basic deal and the way in which it was negotiated are known to be fair. In a major investment for which the host country government may lack competent personnel to protect its interests, the foreign investor might insist that the LDC government retain outside counsel and expert consultants to advise on investment terms. The Harvard Development Advisory Group has advised numerous LDC governments in such matters. Recently it advised the government of Indonesia on a proposed major investment by Alcoa in a new bauxite/aluminum venture. Falconbridge insisted that the government of the Dominican Republic retain a reputable law firm highly experienced in investment matters to assist it in the negotiation of a $185 million investment in nickel mining.

Second, the more diversified and balanced TNC investments are, the less dependence there is on any one host government. Two examples of decreased bargaining power for the TNC as the result of heavy investment concentration in one industry in one country are Jamaican bauxite investments and Chilean copper investments.

Bauxite is considered a strategic material and the United States imports 87 percent of its needs, half from Jamaica. The $650 million U.S. investment in Jamaican bauxite/alumina bulks large in a country of two million people, while the heavy U.S. dependence on one source reduces the companies' bargaining position in the face of Jamaican pressures. In retrospect, the United States and the companies might have been better off if the "second round" investment of $261 million in 1968 had been made in Australia despite the then-existing marginally higher costs involved.

In the mid-1960s, national participation in the Anaconda and Kennecott copper investments had become a major political issue in Chile. At the time Anaconda's response was to double its investment and retain 100 percent ownership. Kennecott, on the other hand, sold 51 percent of its interest to the government of Chile on an installment payment basis. The Kennecott mines were also doubled in size but the expansion was financed in large part by others and Kennecott's equity investment was halved. When nationalization took place Anaconda was far more severely affected than Kennecott, which by then had partly withdrawn from Chile and expanded its business elsewhere.

Third, investment by the World Bank or its subsidiary, the International Finance Corporation (IFC), the Inter-American Development Bank, the Asian Development Bank, or a similar development bank is a valuable way of both internationalizing the investment and establishing its credibility as a fair deal. It is preferable that it be a direct investment in the project, although it may have substantially the same effect if the institution finances an infrastructure development directly related to the private investment.

The $227 million Marinduque nickel mining and refining operation in the Philippines is Filipino-owned with debt financing provided by the IFC and OPIC, with nominal Philippine government participation and extensive debt financing by prospective Japanese customers.

An example of two projects essential to each other's practicability is the location of the $159 million Valco Aluminum Tolling Plant in Ghana because of the large amount of cheap power that would come from the World Bank-financed Volta River Dam and Power Project. Valco is the major purchaser of the electricity generated by the project which also provides power for the industrial development of Ghana and cheap electricity for consumer use. When Ghana moved to nationalize other foreign investments (principally British), it did not move against Valco.

Fourth, the more countries involved in a multinational investment, the more likely it is that the host country will move cautiously. Foreign investors of other countries receive considerable formal and informal support from their governments both bilaterally and through their representatives in international financial institutions such as the World Bank and the Berne Union. The commercial banks of such countries may also be expected to weigh any adverse credit implications of expropriatory acts without compensation in making their loan decisions.

While the $132 million foreign commitment in the Boke aluminum operation in Guinea is largely American and Canadian, there is French (10 percent), German (10 percent), and Italian (6 percent) participation. Most of these investments are insured against expropriation by their respective government insurance organizations or else consist of export loans by government credit institutions of the investors' home countries. In the case of the $150 million Freeport copper mine in Indonesia, United States, Japanese, and German companies are not only the investors but also the purchasers of the entire output. The investors, who are important factors in their national copper industries, may be expected to have additional power to resist unacceptable treatment by the Indonesian government because of their role as purchasers.

Fifth, debt investment is less contentious than equity investment. The valuation of equity is comparatively difficult and susceptible to different formulas to determine compensation whereas the repayment features of debt are agreed in advance. Moreover, since the debt instrument specifies amount, dates of repayment, interest rates, and a designated payee, default becomes clear immediately and may concern other creditors who are important to the host country's continuing cash flow needs. In the case of Kennecott's Chilean investment, although the government of Chile tried to repudiate some of its debt, the amount of the obligation was not in question and the problem associated with the debt of Sociedad El Teniente, S.A., to the Braden Copper Company, a Kennecott subsidiary, was an inability to repay. On the other hand, the value of the Kennecott equity in the same property has been the subject of contention.

Sometimes contractual arrangements can be substituted for an equity investment. In certain export situations where the prospective investor is primarily concerned with assuring a source of supply, "take or pay" contracts may be preferable to an equity investment. The question of "ownership" is precluded, yet a firm contract provides a basis for obtaining financing. In a Far Eastern country, for example, a major United States user of metal negotiated a "take or pay" supply contract with an enterprise owned by European nationals. The credit-worthiness of the buyer and the firmness of the contract made the contract sufficient collateral for the debt financing required.

Sixth, in negotiating the terms of an investment to produce items for export the investor may arrange foreign exchange protection in a less onerous form than a flat convertibility agreement. The

Freeport copper agreement with the government of Indonesia, for instance, provides that export earnings be deposited abroad in a trust administered by a third party who distributes the funds in accordance with the agreed formula. Hard currency is assured to meet dividend and debt service requirements.

Seventh, it is important to try in advance to eliminate potential sources of conflict and to establish the steps to be taken if disputes arise. Mechanisms might include contractual provisions for international arbitration, such as referral to the International Center for the Settlement of Investment Disputes (ICSID), and a formula to determine the fair market price of the product, or fact-finding and conciliation arrangements.

Though there is no supranational forum that can bind sovereign governments, legitimacy as a moral force should not be ignored. ICSID has had only two disputes referred to it since its organization in 1966. The Alcoa agreement with the government of Jamaica provided that disputes arising from the investment agreement be referred to ICSID. It remains unclear whether the government of Jamaica can prevent referral of its effort to renegotiate the terms of the investment.

The government of Botswana and AMAX stipulated in their investment agreement that the price of the copper/nickel matte produced by the mine be adjusted by a formula based on the prices quoted on the London Metal Exchange. Firestone Tire was able to arrange tariff protection for five years for its Kenyan investment because the existing market was too small to support more than one company.

Eighth, the foreign investor should be politically nonpartisan. Being identified as partisan in the LDC may have undesirable consequences should the government change. In certain major investments, it is advisable to obtain additional assurances at the highest level in the host country that the proposed project is fully familiar and welcome to both the government leaders and opposition party leaders. Such assurances should be given in public statements, preferably in the host country legislature, or, alternatively, in a declaration to the press. Botswana and Jamaica, for example, have provided such assurances.

Ninth, consideration may be given to joint ventures with local investors in the LDC. Joint ventures and divestiture have often been advocated as panaceas to mitigate economic nationalist pressures in the LDC, but the consensus of U.S. embassies is that such decisions are best made on a case-by-case basis.

Local capital for a significant equity participation in a major investment is scarce. The only source of capital may be members of the local oligopoly of the LDC government itself, and many are already short of capital or have strained their credit.

Joint ventures between investors of disproportionate economic strength may not make for an amicable relationship. Disparities can cause differences between the partners on such fundamentals as the rate of return expected, the portion of earnings to be reinvested, dividends, and proper cost allocations for the foreign investor's parent company support capabilities. The joint venture agreement should state in detail the arrangements between the investors, particularly formulas for transfer-pricing and other dealings between the local enterprise and the foreign investor's parent company and its subsidiaries.

Joint ventures with LDC partners sometimes require minimal equity and heavy debt, creating an imbalanced financial structure. The resulting debt-equity ratio may possibly be difficult for the enterprise to sustain readily and make it vulnerable to short-term losses or unanticipated over-run costs.

A final problem that can arise in joint ventures is that the local partner may become a political target of the LDC government. Nevertheless, under proper conditions, a joint venture may be eminently desirable and may even be mandatory as a condition of entry to the LDC. The principal contribution of the local partner is apt to be knowledge of the local scene to guide conduct in an alien culture.

Divestiture presents many of the same problems as joint ventures but has the advantage of undiluted single control of the enterprise, at least during the early years. An example of a successful divestiture is that of the $7 million ITT investment in a satellite earth communications station in Indonesia. ITT agreed to finance and construct the facility and then turn the title over to the government of Indonesia in return for a contract to operate and manage the station. The earnings were split 50-50.

The Andean Pact countries wish to have pre-agreed terms of divestiture which to be attractive must allow the foreign investor to amortize his investment and obtain a fair return during his tenure. Pre-agreed divestiture may, however, tempt the foreign investor to maximize short-term profits without regard to subsequent cost by, for example, skimping on maintenance costs or long-term management development efforts.

Tenth, the management of the TNC can consider the purchase of expropriation insurance. In 1973, 14 governments provided such insurance for their nationals. Foremost among them was the U.S. government through OPIC. Investment insurance may be helpful during the inception and the implementation of a direct foreign investment and may be vital in the event of expropriation.

Insurers as well as investors can reduce the risk of bilateral disputes through diversification. In 1974, under Lloyd's leadership, British and continental European private insurance companies reinsured part of OPIC's expropriation liability, which could be as much as $54 million in any one year; and the Berne Union, a 40-year-old international association of national export credit organizations, assumed political risk insurance problems as well. Failure of a host country to live up to its obligations will quickly become known in the international credit community and may adversely affect its credit worthiness.

Bilateral country agreements regarding OPIC investments are negotiated in advance with the host LDC. The U.S. agreement with the host country is designed to establish a procedure for settlement of disputes rather than formally commit the host government to respect the rights of the investor.

Before entering into an expropriation risk contract, OPIC applies criteria designed to estimate the long-term effects of a proposed investment, in the belief that a preponderantly beneficial effect on the LDC will tend to preserve peaceful possession by the investor of his property and to further the interest of both the LDC and the United States. The analysis may reveal project weaknesses which might be troublesome later and which can be corrected by restructuring the project. In any case, it is wiser to face up to the probable effects before the fact than after trouble develops.

OPIC uses its specialized expertise to help achieve a settlement between the TNC and the LDC without political confrontation, an outcome in which it has a real interest because of its financial stake. OPIC independently attempts to determine the facts and judge the merits of a dispute and may audit the financial statements of the insured U.S. investor and the foreign enterprise to determine the amount of the insured investment or may employ technical experts to verify the assertions of either the U.S. investor or the LDC concerning various aspects of the dispute.

OPIC consults with the investor, the State Department, the Treasury, and any other government agencies concerned and serves in the special interagency group established under the Council on International Economic Policy. OPIC prefers not to deal directly with the host country government but to communicate its position through the State Department. OPIC frequently provides information and advice to State Department representatives in Washington and the field.

Through its broad authority to settle claims, OPIC may use its guaranty to assist the LDC in paying compensation. Its presence and findings may therefore contribute to more pragmatic bargaining between the LDC and the company and thereby lessen ideological confrontation. Despite OPIC capabilities, there are definite limitations on the extent to which it can influence positions that have hardened or situations in which the dispute has become a highly politicized local issue.

Under OPIC insurance contracts the investor must pursue local administrative and judicial remedies, prove the value of the insured investment according to accepted U.S. accounting principles, and not act in a way that would endanger the investment. The investor also commits himself to wait one year from the date of the expropriation for his claim to mature, to negotiate in good faith with the LDC for a satisfactory settlement, to keep OPIC fully advised of his efforts to achieve a settlement, and not to make a binding settlement without OPIC's prior consent.

OPIC and its predecessors have insured some 3,000 projects in 80 countries against political risk. Its own expropriation exposure, including other uninsured investment, was about $2.5 billion in August 1974. Not only does OPIC have experience in project analysis but it also has the dubious honor of having had by far more pragmatic expropriation dispute experience than any company or other government agency, whether U.S. or foreign. As of September 15, 1974, OPIC had made determinations on a total of twenty-three expropriation claims of which fifteen claims were paid, four claims withdrawn by the investor, and four claims denied. Three of the denied claims were submitted to arbitration in accordance with provisions of the insurance contract; OPIC was upheld in one arbitration and the other two were pending.

The obvious first capability of OPIC is reimbursement of an investor whose property has been expropriated without compensation. Besides receiving the cash equivalent of the net insured investment the investor also will have a full investigation made by an agency of the U.S. government to establish the shortfall, if any, between the compensation paid and the insured net investment.

Bethlehem Steel's iron ore project was one of the first mines seized by the government of Chile in early 1971. When the Chilean government offered compensation at less than book value, OPIC, which had insured a portion of the investment, exercised its contractual right to refuse to consent to the proposed settlement. Further negotiations ultimately obtained an agreement to pay book value with the condition that OPIC shift its political risk insurance of the Bethlehem equity to cover a portion of the promissory notes issued by the government of Chile.

The Kennecott debt referred to earlier is of interest here. In December 1972, OPIC settled the claim of a subsidiary of Kennecott Copper Corporation which held notes issued by the El Teniente Mine and guaranteed by an agency of the Chilean government with a face value of approximately $74 million. OPIC guaranteed the payment of these notes, which were then sold to a trustee for nearly $67 million. The trustee in turn sold participation certificates (also guaranteed by OPIC) in a trust fund composed of these El Teniente notes to certain U.S. financial institutions. In this way Braden (the Kennecott subsidiary) received $67 million to finance its operations and OPIC exchanged a potential $74 million lump sum liability for a contingent liability over a number of years. The Allende government was enabled to abide by international law, which it flouted in various other uninsured cases, and a possible confrontation between the United States and Chile on this issue was avoided.

The one-year waiting period for expropriations to become compensable provides a cooling-off period for the LDC and the investor to reconsider the facts and resolve their differences, if possible. The U.S. government sanctions required by law may be held in abeyance for this year in which the investor is required to pursue his local legal remedies and to attempt to negotiate in good faith with the LDC government. In Bolivia, for example, a change in government occurred during the waiting period and the new government was more favorably disposed to work out an installment payment agreement to compensate the investors.

OPIC's strategy is to keep the investor "out front" in negotiations with the LDC. This reduces the possibility of government-to-government confrontation in the early stages of a dispute and allows time for the complex facts concerning an investment to become available. OPIC's power to withhold its consent from an agreed settlement has often deferred the expropriation or has secured substantially better terms. OPIC can also obtain a satisfactory settlement in disputes where the investor cannot. In a case involving the expropriation of a fish processing and freezing operation in Somalia, OPIC was able to negotiate a compensation agreement directly with the government of Somalia after the investor had failed to do so and had been paid by OPIC.

Bargaining between the host LDC and the TNC is a continual process. Before any investment commitment it should begin to establish a mutual understanding of the constituency needs of the government and the profit needs of the company. Though an investment agreement with a sovereign government is primarily a memorandum of understanding because it is difficult to enforce, informed negotiation is nevertheless the first step in dispute prevention. Constructive attitudes and friendly relationships developed over the initial bargaining period may be profoundly influential over the years.

For the TNC to reduce the risk of renegotiation, nationalization, or expropriation and to retain freedom to operate, there should be a major new management function ranking in importance with marketing, production, and sales. Efforts should be made to develop good relationships with officials in the LDC. Senior government officials feel that the officers of the parent company are their counterparts; consequently, a senior management officer responsible for company-wide policy-making should participate in discussion with the LDC government, the U.S. government, and other institutions. The establishment of working relationships between the TNC and the middle level government officials who frequently do staff work on issues for higher level policy-makers can also aid mutual understanding.

In the early period, the prospective benefits fuel the efforts of both TNC and LDC to work closely together to bring forth a viable proposal. At some point in mining and other large fixed-asset investments, the conditions negotiated by both parties are embodied in a written instrument intended to be binding, except for minor variations caused by interpretation of language when applied to actual working conditions. In some cases, such as the Andean countries, even "ultimate" future conditions of TNC investment are spelled out in advance.

Once the investor has gone beyond the point of no return, relative bargaining strengths may change substantially. No agreement can cover all contingencies, and wide latitude remains for the application of LDC power. Because of personal, bureaucratic, or national considerations, the various agencies of the LDC government may exercise their powers in a way that differs substantially from the expectations of the investor, possibly to the point of coerced renegotiation or nationalization. The foreign investor has no reliable means of appeal in such circumstances and stands committed by its irrevocable outlay of money to work out such differences as best it can or abandon its investment and write off its loss.

The United States government may also be involved in the negotiating process. The fact of collaboration between the government and American investors is sometimes seen as a demonstration that big business shapes U.S. policy for its own ends. This suspicion in the United States and in the LDCs must be allayed if the United States is to maintain, let alone increase, its world market share and preserve economic health at home.

Collaboration should connote the joint effort of parties with separate but parallel interests working together. This collaboration must begin at the inception of the investment and extend through the entire investment cycle, including possible U.S. government protection in the event of an unresolved dispute. Joint consultation in the investment decisions should facilitate the selection of sound investments and assist their implementation and operation. If a dispute does develop, the objective should be to avoid confrontation and to buy time for the merits of the dispute to be judged by the international credit community.

Government and private sector must be mutually supportive. Business and government are closely associated in other industrialized competitors of the United States such as Germany and Japan, and they are vigilant in the joint pursuit and protection of their mutual foreign business opportunities. The United States too has national interests in foreign investments, whether economic, political, or strategic. A satisfactory settlement of investment disputes must assure that U.S. government interests are met as well as those of the investors.

Toward the Future

There is strong political pressure on states to use their sovereign power to reallocate economic resources, either foreign or domestic, for national purposes which may conflict with growing economic interdependency. While domestic political pressures may generate increasing nationalism, global population, food, fuel, and monetary problems indicate the transnational nature of the economic process. The futility of dealing any longer with such issues on a national basis may be evident, but international institutions do not yet have the capability and authority to provide an alternative.

Sovereign states can limit the TNC through their domination of economic activity within their borders, but by careful planning and continuous attention the TNC may reconcile its interests with those of both host and home countries. Nevertheless, should their interests conflict, the home country government must be prepared to determine its own legitimate interest in the foreign investment, the merits of its foreign investors' grievances against arbitrary actions of host governments, and what actions it may reasonably take.

The new methods of coerced divestiture or renegotiation of investment terms experienced in LDCs are closely related to rapidly changing reinterpretations of traditional views of property rights and the sanctity of contractual agreements. At one time management and equity capital were seemingly inextricably intertwined. It is now management and government who appear to be most involved with each other.

We are in the midst of a redefinition of the roles of "private" enterprise and government. Despite the interdependence of the two, governments will tend to finance their increasing social responsibilities by allocating a greater share of the gross revenues of enterprises in various ways. For example, taxes may be increased, safety and environmental standards raised, and higher product quality required. Regardless of the method used, the net effect will be to diminish the portion of the firm's gross revenues to be shared out among the firm's own constituencies—shareholders, customers, supplier, financiers, management, and labor.

Just as government must seek out ways of meeting practical political needs through practicable economic measures, the TNC must develop practicable political ways of meeting its economic needs. The question is not any longer whether governments and TNCs should be involved with each other, but how best to conduct that relationship. It appears that the private or mixed enterprise must develop adequate responses to its own entrepreneurial demands within the larger strategy of the state.

Traditional rituals and dogmas appear increasingly ineffective. A broader advance understanding of the mutual need for political and economic co-existence is essential for a creative approach to risk management. Selectivity in the initial investment can mitigate future problems of protection. In addition, certain measures can be incorporated in the investment agreement, but they are subject to ongoing bargaining and renegotiation. Expertise in investment selection and protection is developing in both the LDCs and the industrialized countries, where the number of national political risk insurance programs has grown from four to fourteen in the six years since 1968. International consultation is still in an initial period of development and perhaps IIIA or ICSID will still emerge as an effective force.

The objective must be a new synthesis that will preserve the ability of a market-directed economy to meet the needs of a centrally directed political structure. Joint definition and consequent clarification of parallel interests should make it possible for the TNC to demonstrate that it is the most effective tool to achieve effective development and maximum productivity.

Eugene V. Rostow

8

The Multinational Corporation
and the Future of the World Economy

That the income growth is widening between the rich countries and the poor ones is one of the sad but irrefutable facts of modern life, and that gap may well become wider under increasing pressure from demography and the growing scarcity of material. This calls for a massive movement of capital and of business from the industrialized to the developing nations through multinational companies, yet that cannot be achieved without major institutional changes.

G. W. B.

The perspective of this chapter is a problem which public and political opinion is only beginning to perceive as a predicate for policy rather than a rhetorical flourish: the growing disparity in income between the rich industrialized countries and most of the developing nations. It is safe to assume that even the bulge in the prices of petroleum and some other raw materials which became manifest in 1973 will not basically alter the situation in the long run, save perhaps for a few developing nations particularly favored by geology. On the contrary, for many developing nations without oil of their own, like India, the disparity can be expected to become worse.

A widening gulf between the rich countries and the poor ones is a profound wrong in itself, and an untenable basis for peaceful relations among the members of the world community. If it continues at its present level, or becomes worse, it will precipitate vast migrations of people from the stagnant economies of many developing nations to the industrialized countries, which have been close to full employment for most of the period since 1947, and can be expected to restore that state of affairs, more or less successfully, in the near future. Unless we can somehow organize a flow of capital, technology, and entrepreneurship from the industrialized to the developing countries, on a scale far larger than any achieved thus far, the chronic shortages of labor in the industrialized world, and the chronic unemployment of the developing nations, will act upon each other like the poles of a magnet, and accelerate the movement of people from Africa, Asia, and some Latin American countries to the centers of industrialization. The pressures for such a movement of peoples are of course intensified by the worldwide pattern of demographic trends, and by modern facilities for transportation and communication, which stimulate, and make possible, much that was impossible before.

But a vast and nearly uncontrollable migration of peoples from South to North would generate destructive social and political conflict, both within the industrialized nations, and between them and the developing countries. Small-scale portents of this sort are visible in many parts of the world already—those focusing on the Algerians in France; the Greeks and Turks in Germany and the Netherlands; the Pakistanis, Indians, Moroccans, and West Indians in Great Britain; the Haitians in Canada; and, in the United States, the two million illegal immigrants a year arriving from Mexico. It is not difficult to imagine the reactions these movements would catalyze, if they were to be increased in size by a factor of 10, 20, or 100.

There are only two ways in which the growing disparity of income between the rich and most of the poor countries can be overcome: by the movement of unemployed or underemployed labor from the developing nations to the industrial ones, or by a movement of capital and entrepreneurship from the industrialized nations to the developing world. There are no alternative choices. In the long run, or even the moderately short run, the first approach would result in an explosion of xenophobia in the industrialized world. The second is therefore the only principle for policy which is compatible with our humanity, our interests, and our hopes for a peaceful and progressive future.

Two hundred years of experience with the industrial revolution should make it clear that modernization is a complex sociological process. Both European and non-European cultures have succeeded in mastering the secrets of modern wealth. Many have failed. I start with the axiom, which I shall not attempt to demonstrate here, that the task of modernization is beyond the capacity of even the most efficient governments of the developing nations on a genuinely socialist basis. Many, of course, are and will continue to be hopelessly inefficient. But even the Soviet Union and the socialist countries of Eastern Europe—with the possible exception of East Germany—rely increasingly on the decentralized decision-making of the market mechanism, and, in recent years, on foreign capital and entrepreneurship as well. I believe that all the developing nations, however socialist in ideology, will have to depend more and more upon the private sector if they wish to utilize the labor force available to them, and achieve significant increases in their standard of living. Only a few among the developing countries possess a cadre of entrepreneurs large enough, and well enough trained, to undertake efforts of this magnitude. Even fewer have been able to mobilize their own savings for investment in economic progress. For a long time to come, therefore, the developing countries will have to attract foreign capital and foreign entrepreneurship if they wish to improve the standard of living of their people.

For these reasons, the argument is that the successful negotiation of an international treaty which could facilitate a massive movement of capital and of business from the industrialized to the developing nations through "multinational" companies is among the most urgent tasks of diplomacy. If we dare to assume that the fragile structure of imperfect peace which has been achieved at great cost since 1945, and the integrated international economy which developed within that framework, can somehow be restored and renewed—strenuous assumptions for anyone writing in 1974—

the multinational company should be one of the most important institutions of international stability and progress for at least the next twenty-five years.

I cannot reach a conclusion as to which facet of the problem thus far has been the most poignant comment on the prevalence of folly among us: the fact that the governments of most of the developing countries are doubtful or suspicious about the idea of such a treaty, as the entering wedge for a policy of "Imperialism"; or the fact that most of the governments of the industrialized nations have been equally dubious, for a number of equally mythical reasons quite as hostile to their own interests.

The development of the world economy since World War II is an extraordinary achievement in itself. The continued development of that economy as a system is essential to the possibility of narrowing the gap between the rich and the poor nations. Economic forces, like those of security, are integrating the world, not dividing it into regional blocs. The centripetal pressures for economic integration are far stronger than those of separatism and multipolarity.

The liberal economic policies launched by Presidents Roosevelt and Truman—the policies represented by Bretton Woods, GATT, the Marshall Plan, and the programs of national and international assistance to the developing nations—precipitated a nearly miraculous process of cumulative development in many parts of the world. The success of those policies has brought about a new situation requiring new measures and indeed new institutions if the world is to avoid a retreat into autarchy or worse.

Through twenty-five years of imaginative cooperation, the bankers, businessmen, trade unions, economists, and governments of Western Europe, North America, and Japan created an economic system of a kind which had been unknown since 1914: a closely unified economy of the industrialized nations. That economy functions as the nucleus of a far-reaching and progressive Western economic order, embracing many smaller industrialized nations, and large parts of the Third World as well. It is rapidly drawing the economies of many communist nations into its orbit.

The economic pressures for closer and closer association are not confined to the circle of rich capitalist nations in the Northern

Hemisphere. China has sought to enter the circle, for fundamental reasons of national security. And even the Soviet Union seems divided, as has happened several times in the past, between the advantages of economic cooperation with the West and the appeal of its national and ideological ambitions. It has sought credits to finance the purchase of machinery and technology from the United States—and of course it has bought grain on an extremely large scale. Thus far, however, it has been unwilling to make even the minimal political concessions without which such economic relations will remain beyond its reach.

The Western economic system is both planned and decentralized: directed, but also flexible. It is planned through the use of fiscal and monetary policies to maintain high levels of demand. And it is decentralized through its reliance on the responses of competitive markets to economic opportunities. For all its problems and shortcomings, the international Western economy has proved to be by far the most successful of all the economic systems now functioning in the world. It has raised living standards, and promoted a wide dispersal of power and opportunity. And, in countries which desired to pursue such goals, it has proved to be the solid foundation for a humane social order as well.

The fundamental economic problem which has emerged in the development of the Western international economy is structural. The economies of Western Europe, North America, and Japan are being integrated at an accelerating rate by irreversible flows of trade, capital, entrepreneurship, tourism, technology, and security expenditures. They have become a single economy in practice. But their economic activities are now more completely and effectively integrated than their institutions for economic control, and particularly their institutions for monetary management. Purely national monetary institutions and policies have lost their capacity to govern the economic relations among the key nations themselves, and their collective relations with many other nations, notably, but not exclusively, with the nations producing oil. The sheer volume of transfers required by the scale and complexity of international economic transactions today makes it impossible to manage monetary policy through a few phone calls and swaps among the central bankers, and an occasional secret weekend at agreeable country houses in France or Britain. Such methods worked well between 1945 and 1971. They collapsed in 1971 because of human mistakes, and, more fundamentally, because they were no longer adequate to the magnitude of the problem. Strong social and political forces rebelled against constraint. The integrated Western economy lacked a gyroscope. It had become more and more vulnerable.

This structural weakness of the Western economic system—its failure thus far to establish workable machinery for collective monetary management—is the principal reason why inflation has become so endemic, and so dangerous, even in the relatively stable societies of the industrialized nations.

A second trend has reinforced this vulnerability: Keynesism. After World War II, all the democratic nations practiced Keynesism, even if they professed other ideologies. Their governments and central banks used monetary and fiscal policy to maintain high levels of employment by offsetting fluctuations in the level of private expenditure. My purpose here is not to criticize this development, or to propose that we return to our older habits of treating the trade cycle as a visitation of nature or of God. It is rather to point out that we still have much to learn about the art of Keynesian policy. We are only at the beginning of this new phase of economic policy-making, at least as a contemporary phenomenon. And we are only beginning to realize how complex an organism a modern economy is, and how difficult it is to predict or control its responses to a given set of changes in the direction and volume of spending. The economic order, as we see only too clearly now, is not a mathematical model governed by a computer.

By the mid-fifties, all the democratic societies had developed an inflationary bias, which became steadily more pronounced as the public came to believe in the efficacy of Keynesian measures, and adjusted their anticipations accordingly. Many students of the problem warned against the inflationary potential of some Keynesian programs as early as the late 1950s. By 1970 widespread alarm had developed about the accelerating trend toward inflation. Our alarm was addressed to trends which would now seem trivial. But we were right. With some variation among countries, the pace of inflation in the OECD group as a whole rose from 2.6 percent per year between 1955 and 1960 and 2.7 percent per year between 1960 and 1965 to 4.3 percent per year between 1965 and 1970. After 1970, of course, the rate was much higher, and darted forward at a dizzying pace after October 1973.

Wage policy—and tax policy as well—are among the major causes of the inflationary bias of economic policy in the Keynesian era. We often hear it said that rising money wages are "inflationary." The usage conceals the real problem. If money wage rates or other direct costs rise, while income remains constant, output will fall. No one has yet succeeded in repealing the principle of the elasticity of demand. Output can be maintained only if prices rise in proportion to the increase of direct costs, and rise to a level of profit high enough to justify investment. And such price increases, offsetting the increases in direct costs, can be achieved only by inflationary increases in the flow of money expenditures. The true root of inflation is always on the money side of the equation. Without monetary expansion, high-wage bargains and other high-direct-cost bargains could not be validated; the increases in price simply could not occur.

For this reason, Keynes himself argued that the only way in which a democratic society could sustain a policy of full employment was on the solid foundation of fixed money wage rates. In such a regime, he contended, prices would fall gradually as productivity increased, and full employment would put no strain on the balance of payments.

It goes without saying that we have not yet accepted Keynes' conclusion, or anything near it, as a rule of policy. I should not be surprised, however, to see the democratic trade unions of the Western countries come close to Keynes' view in the near future. Working people have been badly hurt by inflation. They have long since seen through the "money illusion." And they are profoundly concerned about the adequacy of their pensions and other welfare arrangements.

The inability of any country thus far to maintain a wage and tax policy compatible with full employment at stable prices is not the only factor accelerating the process of inflation in recent years.

Certain key countries, and especially the United States, broke the rules of the system on a large and destructive scale. Even before the oil crisis of 1973–1974, they indulged in altogether excessive rates of domestic and international inflation. They were unable or unwilling to adopt the measures which are necessary to the workability of the balance of payments adjustment process. These excesses destroyed the Bretton Woods system in 1971. The level of uncertainty about the future of exchange rates, and of inflation, therefore increased. Interest rates rose in consequence. And the international economy, already vulnerable to shock for the reasons I have tried to identify, became even more vulnerable.

Thus the sharp rise in oil prices and the prices of other raw materials in recent years was superimposed on an international system already near the breaking point. The worldwide process of industrialization and development and the general inflationary boom of 1971–73 had led to a rapid increase in the demand for petroleum and other raw materials. That increase in demand became feverish as the pool of Eurodollars grew from $30 billion to $80 billion in less than three years. The upward pressure on world raw material and other prices was highly visible well before the October war in 1973. But the drastic price increases of the oil producing states, launched concurrently with that war, precipitated not a panicky or a euphoric acceptance of inflation, such as the reactions generated by some inflations of the past, but a resigned and nearly lethargic response, as if there were nothing to do in the face of these problems but meekly to submit.

All these trends point in the same direction: the necessity for the key industrialized nations, and for the OECD nations as a group, to take joint action in the monetary sphere. A few of our financial leaders have been urging this course for some time. Hopefully, the situation is now bad enough to persuade even our hesitant governments to act.

What is required, as a first step, is the joint management of reserves through a small institution: an account, a clearing union, a central bank. The name is not important. But the function is extremely important. Unless we do this there is nothing else we can do effectively. No economy can function without a central bank.

The kind of bank I have in mind could help to concert and harmonize the economic policies of the key nations. It should stabilize their relations with each other, and provide a firm foundation for their relations of trade and investment with the developing nations. It should strengthen the hand of discipline, and thus make it easier to achieve discipline in all the participating countries. And it is the only possible beginning for a policy which could permit the OECD nations to deal sensibly and as equals with the oil producers' cartel, in order to reach understandings about the terms of trade which will permit the world economy, on which all depend, to function once again.

The reasons I should advance for these propositions are implicit in what I have said already. The degree of integration among the economies of the key industrial nations, and the extent of their interdependence with many other nations, developed and developing alike, has meant that no one economy, not even that of the United States or of the European Community, has genuine autonomy. No solutions are possible unless Europe, North America, and Japan act together. Each nation has the same interest in the continued viability of the Western economic system as a system, multilateral in its trade policy, and based on the free movement of capital and the convertibility of currencies. The system as a whole has to rally if one member or another experiences difficulty. Everyone's interest in the outcome is the same. The nations are far more cohesive in economic affairs than they realize consciously—far more cohesive than the atmosphere of their newspapers or politics might suggest. For each knows, at some level of instinct, that unless the progressive international economy of the Bretton Woods period is adapted to new conditions, and restored, there is no chance for any of our nations to grow, or indeed even to prosper. If the monetary system continues to disintegrate, the liberal trading rules which have proved to be in everyone's interest during the last twenty-five years will follow, and we shall be driven to retreat into autarchy, depression, and perhaps worse.

Logic of this order has dominated our affairs since the beginning of the postwar period, when the United States consciously redistributed its reserves. Without that action—which treated monetary

reserves as a common resource—the restoration of convertibility in
Europe and Japan would have been impossible. We have all acted
in this pattern ever since, through swaps, through the gold pool
operations, and most recently through the German loans to Italy.

The special dilemmas of the oil problem simply reinforce the
arguments for this line of policy. At the moment, the OECD nations
as a group are running balance of payments deficits on an
unimaginable scale in order to pay for their current consumption of
petroleum. Unless this process is stopped, and stopped abruptly, our
nations will have transferred control of their economies—wealth,
that is to say, and power in one of its most significant forms—to the
oil producing countries, where it could be seized by any passing
buccaneer.

Some contend that if only these petrodollars are deposited on
medium or long term in the banks of New York, Frankfurt,
London, and Amsterdam, all will be well. It is hard to imagine
policies so blind. The recycling remedy, however necessary by way
of transition, would not even apply a tourniquet to the patient's
arm. At this writing, however, this seems to be all the policy we
have. I can detect no massive shift of freight and passengers to the
railroads, or even the buses; no burst of research and development
on the use of substitute fuels; no rationing or other radical programs
of conservation.

The nature of the problem determines the outline of the most
appropriate remedy. The problem is to restore the Western
economy to a position in which it could pay for its energy imports
out of current income, not capital, and at the same time preserve
and even strengthen the system as an entity. The several countries
of the OECD group are in different positions with regard to energy
supplies. Yet, as they have finally agreed, all must function
together. Even when they have launched excellent programs of
conservation, sharing, and substitution, the OECD nations as a
group will require very large extra sums of hard money for at least
another ten years in order to pay for oil at anything like its present
or prospective price. To obtain that amount out of current income,
the OECD nations would have to increase their net trade or
payments surplus, calculated without the oil item, by something

like 1.5 percent or 2 percent of their Gross National Product. It should be possible to accomplish this goal—and indeed to do so out of growth, rather than by reducing standards of living—if the OECD nations genuinely consolidate their monetary systems, manage their reserves together, and on that footing develop and carry out concerted economic policies which renew the economic and social momentum of the 1950s and 1960s.

The consolidation of the Western banking machinery is desirable for many other reasons. In the perspective of the oil problem, however, it is quite simply indispensable.

This principle—that of restoring the basic balance of payments surplus of the OECD nations as a group—is vital in many other perspectives. On such a footing, and only on such a footing, the industrialized nations could continue to carry out their obligations to help modernize the economies of what we have begun to call the countries of the Fourth World—that is, the developing countries which lack oil, sugar, or some other raw material currently selling at very high prices. That kind of investment looms up as one of the major problems of world society during the years ahead. Unless the developing nations are modernized, we face the impossible prospect of a world more sharply divided than ever between rich and poor.

A large-scale new movement of private capital, entrepreneurship, and management to the developing nations is already proceeding, and proceeding rapidly. It is the key to the development process in Brazil, Mexico, Taiwan, Israel, Iran, Malaysia, Hong Kong, Singapore, Indonesia, and many other nations which are success- fully raising their standards of living as full participants in the international Western economy. Various proposals have been put forward in recent years for international agreements through which the developing countries—and indeed all countries—could be assured a larger and more regular flow of private capital and entrepreneurship. The prompt negotiation and conclusion of a multilateral treaty that could achieve this goal, on fair and agreed terms, is one of the most important tasks for world statesmanship. The growth of most of the developing countries is inconceivable without it. So is the future of the industrial nations.

J. S. Nye and Seymour J. Rubin

9

The Longer Range Political Role
of the Multinational Corporation

As institutions which control a significant share of world resources, multinational corporations necessarily command considerable power. They have now become a sufficient world force that it is essential to try to determine where they fit in a rational world order. Professor Nye addresses himself to that question in the following chapter.

G. W. B.

J. S. N.: Multinational Corporations and World Order

There is an apparent paradox in the political importance of the multinational corporation. Something between two hundred and three hundred large multinational enterprises or clusters of corporations joined together by common ownership and management strategy, operate simultaneously in twenty or more different

JOSEPH S. NYE, JR., *is Professor of Government at Harvard University. He has been a visiting fellow at the Royal Institute of International Affairs. A governor of the Atlantic Institute, Dr. Nye has been an editor of* International Organization *and a director of the U.N. Association. He has written many books and articles on politics and international organizations.*

nations.[1] Some observers believe that by the end of the century three hundred giant corporations will account for a large majority of world industrial production, and that the economic sovereignty of nation-states is obsolete. Yet despite the fact that the three billion dollars of value added annually to product by each of the top ten multinationals was greater than the gross national product of some eighty member states of the United Nations, even weak states can and sometimes have nationalized the local affiliate of a multinational corporation.

There is nothing new about the existence of multinational corporations. What is new is the political attention that they are receiving. For example, a Canadian editor recalls discussing American direct investment in Canada with Ambassador Livingston Merchant in 1956, and agreeing that whatever the problems, it was "not a question involving intergovernmental relations." Today the activities of multinational corporations are a major issue in relations between the two governments, and among governments more broadly. The economists' antiseptic references to "direct investment" have been supplemented, and often supplanted, by references to "multinational corporations" with implicit political connotations of private power and threats to national autonomy. These political connotations, as much as their economic importance, have led to increased concern about the implications of multinational corporations for world order and an increasing involvement of international organizations, including the United Nations.

In July 1972, the U.N. Economic and Social Council passed a resolution requesting that the Secretary-General appoint a "group of eminent persons" to study the role of multinational corporations in international relations and the process of development. Of the twenty persons appointed, eight came from less developed countries, two from Communist countries, and ten from the "rich" countries, including two Americans, Senator Jacob Javits of New York and J. Irwin Miller, Chairman of Cummins Engine Company. During

---

[1] The number of multinationals can be set as high as 7,300 if one foreign affiliate is set as the criterion. See *Multinational Corporations in World Development*, ST/ECA/190 (New York, 1973). While the term enterprise is more strictly accurate, the term "multinational corporation" has become the common term.

1973, the group heard testimony from corporate presidents, professors, trade unionists, and general social critics. In the summer of 1974, the group presented its report. Its three main recommendations were: (1) the establishment of a U.N. Commission on Multinational Corporations which, among other things would work out codes of conduct; (2) creation of an Information and Research Center on Multinational Corporations as part of the U.N. Secretariat; and (3) a number of specific steps including technical assistance designed to strengthen the bargaining position of less developed countries vis-à-vis multinational corporations.

Even this modest degree of agreement was difficult to achieve. The "clarifying" comments by nine of the twenty members of the group fill some sixty pages, or nearly half the report. Nevertheless, as J. Irwin Miller commented, the report is valuable because it "reflects much of the present (confused) state of thinking about multinational corporations, and it probably covers most of those actions which might be usefully undertaken now by nations and by the international community."

The critical comments indicate that one of the major areas of confusion was about how, and to what extent, multinational corporations could be considered to have a role in world politics. The International Chamber of Commerce has similarly criticized the report because it "wrongly attributes political power to these enterprises and grossly understates the power of sovereign governments."

Part of the problem in understanding the political role of multinationals stems from the tendency to think of international politics in overly restricted terms. Traditionally "realists" have tended to think of international politics as a political-military struggle among states with force as the major instrument of power and military security the dominant concern. Recent years, however, have seen subtle shifts in the goals which nations pursue in world politics and the instruments they use to achieve these goals. Economic and welfare-oriented objectives have increased in prominence at the same time that military force has become somewhat less dominant.

Nuclear technology and changing domestic values have made the use of military force a more costly option for the governments of the advanced industrial societies. While this is not equally true for all states (and not at all true for some non-state groups), there are large areas of interstate politics where force is not a useful instrument. As Mark Twain remarked of a notice of his death, pronouncements regarding the total obsolescence of military force are "premature." In the last resort military force dominates other means of power. In extreme situations, force is necessary to guarantee national survival. But much of international politics is not extreme and not about survival, and in these areas military force is far too blunt and costly an instrument to be useful. While force retains an important role in military deterrence, it is often inappropriate as an instrument for the achievement of positive goals, particularly in the economic relations among advanced industrial societies. A threat of bombardment may have helped the U.S. to induce Japan to trade a century ago, but it was not a useful instrument in the recent struggle over the value of the yen.

Along with the increased costliness and diminished efficacy of force has gone a shift in the nature of the problem of national security. The political problem of national security is more than a military matter, and more than a question of mere physical survival. Most peoples demand that their government also assure some minimal expected level of economic welfare; a certain political and social autonomy for the nation; and a degree of national political status. Most national security policies in today's world are designed not merely to insure the physical survival of individuals within national boundaries, but to insure these other objectives as well. Indeed, some national security policies actually increase the risks to physical survival in order to insure greater certainty in enjoyment of economic welfare, political status, and national autonomy.

For many states, the strongest sense of threat has shifted from the military area and territorial integrity to the economic area. Threats to welfare, national autonomy, and long-term national survival seem to arise as much from the economic policies of other states and non-state actors as from hostile military sources. Often such threats are unconventional and unintentional. As John Holmes has described Canada's relations with the United States

> it isn't Washington we have to fear. It is Houston and Pittsburgh and Hollywood. . . . Our fear is not that the U.S. Army will destroy Toronto a second time, but that Toronto will be programmed out of existence by a Texas computer.

In other words, if one broadens his concept of world politics to encompass non-military threats to security and a wider range of sources of power, he quickly sees why multinational corporations have become important in world politics whether they wish it or not. Shifts away from the use of force are shifts away from the area of corporate weakness, and shifts toward greater prominence of economic welfare objectives are shifts in the direction of corporate strength.

It is not enough to reply that most multinationals practice what they preach—"that the business of business is business." Political effects do not depend upon political intentions. The unintentional roles of multinational corporations in world politics are just as important as the intentional roles. For example, when Rumania was unhappy with the prospect of being integrated into an East-European computer scheme, she approached first IBM and later Control Data to produce computers in Rumania. IBM's refusal and CDC's acceptance may have been economically motivated, but the availability of this alternative certainly had political effects for Rumania.

Corporate Roles in Current Political Processes

Generalizations are dangerous. Corporations invest abroad for a variety of reasons. Firms in service industries differ considerably in size and mobility from those in extractive industries or in manufacturing. Even within manufacturing, there are important differences in the bargaining positions at home and abroad of firms whose investments are oriented more toward access to local markets, inexpensive labor, or exploitation of a technological advantage. Moreover, the same firm may have a very different impact on a country with a weak economy and fragmented society than on a country with a balanced economy and stable government. Nonetheless, with these caveats in mind, there are still certain useful generalizations that can be made about the political roles of multinationals.

In general terms, multinational corporations play at least three important roles in the day to day processes of world politics. They help both intentionally and unintentionally, to set the agenda of issues that arise among governments. They serve, usually unintentionally, as instruments of power by which governments (and other groups) try to influence each other. And sometimes they act quite intentionally and quite independently to influence political actors and political structures.

Multinational corporations have affected international politics both directly and indirectly as well as intentionally and unintentionally. In our traditional view of world politics we assume that citizens or corporations affect governments of other countries indirectly through policies they press upon their own government. But citizens and corporations can also affect the governments and politics of other countries by dealing with them directly, quite apart from the activities of their home governments. This transnational political role gives rise to what might be called private foreign policies which co-exist and coalesce with public policies.

DIRECT ROLE: PRIVATE FOREIGN POLICY

Of the three main roles which multinational corporations play in current world politics, the direct transnational role has led to some of the most dramatic examples—witness the case of ITT in Chile, which helped to stimulate both the United States Senate hearings and the creation of the special U.N. group. Yet the dramatic cases may be misleading. A careful case study of foreign corporations in Peru indicates that the trend in corporations' transnational political behavior during this century seems to be *away* from overt involvement. As one observer has noted, "it is ironic that interest in multinational companies is growing at the very time that they are withdrawing from their traditional, more or less overt political role. . . ." [2] The Chilean disclosures are also informative in that ITT was notably unsuccessful in persuading large American based multinational corporations to join them in the direct political role. (It seems that smaller Latin American based firms were less inhibited in their political behavior.) While evidence about the direct role is almost impossible to assemble scientifically, it seems on the basis of disclosures that exist that such cases of major direct political involvement as United Fruit in Guatemala in the 1950s, Union Miniere in Katanga in the 1960s, or ITT in Chile in the 1970s, are a small portion of the state-corporation interactions.

Nonetheless, direct transnational political behavior can be of crucial importance to particular states. Corporations can often translate their economic power into effective political influence. If we conceive of a scale of direct political actions by corporations ranging in descending order of intensity from the hiring of private armies, the bribery of host country soldiers or politicians, campaign contributions to political parties, legitimate lobbying of host government legislators, and advertising to influence the climate of ideas, we undoubtedly find most direct political activities clustered at the lower end of the scale. Corporations may also use economic means (both inducements such as the promises of new investment, and deprivations such as threats of withdrawal) in directly bargaining with governments for such political goals as favorable policies. Sometimes these economic inducements consist of projects not directly related to the corporation's main investment, but designed to create a general reputation of corporate "good citizenship." Just as corporations may have private foreign policies, so one can also think of them as having "private foreign aid policies." [3]

When one considers the direct political role of the corporation in world politics, it is useful to drop the traditional assumption that states always act as coherent entities. If one sees that different groups in societies have different interests and that governments are

---

[2] Charles T. Goodsell, *American Corporations and Peruvian Politics* (Cambridge, Mass., 1974); Louis Turner, "Multinational Companies and the Third World," *The World Today*, Sept. 1974, p. 394.

[3] I am indebted to Andrew Richter for this point and examples from Trinidad.

sometimes alliances of competing bureaucracies pulling in different directions, one can conceive of policy coalitions composed of parts of different governments and corporations. Radicals portray this in terms of the penetration of weak states, or of alliances between central sectors in peripheral states and corporations from central states. Transnational coalitions, however, are not all this simple. For instance, if one looked at the international lobbying that has taken place over a new seabed regime, one found oil companies and some elements of the U.S. government allied with some relatively cohesive poor states against the official U.S. government position. Multinational corporations can affect the coherence of home governments and societies as well as host countries.

Private foreign policies toward host countries may rely upon internal differences within a country or they may treat the country in a more distant fashion. Theodore Moran has illustrated the different strategies by a comparison of Anaconda and Kennecott responses to the impending prospect of Chilean copper nationalization in the late 1960s. Anaconda relied on the local political defense of forming a transnational alliance with the conservative elite in the host country, but to no avail. Kennecott, on the other hand, felt that it was impossible to rely upon traditional political alliances inside a host country and instead worked out a sophisticated external defense based on transnational market and credit networks, so that when nationalization occurred the Chilean government would jeopardize its standing with credit institutions on several continents if it failed to provide adequate compensation. In situations of rising nationalism, the latter strategy may be the safer. In retrospect, Harold Geneen, president of ITT, has argued that

> the answer may be a multinational approach. By this I mean the Germans, the Swiss, the World Bank, and others share in the investment. Then six countries are involved, not one. If something goes wrong, the countries can get tough and do things. You don't go to war, but maybe everybody refuses to give the offending country credits.[4]

[4] See Theodore Moran, "Transnational Strategies of Protection and Defense by Multinational Corporations: Spreading the Risk and Raising the Cost for Nationalization in Natural Resources," *International Organization*, 27 (Spring 1973).

UNINTENDED DIRECT ROLE: INSTRUMENTS OF INFLUENCE

Multinational corporations have also played a direct role in world politics in a second way, not through any political initiative of their own, but as an instrument used by their home or host governments.

The existence of multinational corporations with decision domains crossing several national boundaries has provided an additional instrument for governments to attempt to use in their relations with each other. For example, the United States has attempted through extraterritorial control of the trading relations of affiliates of U.S.-based corporations to extend its foreign policy embargoes into the jurisdiction of other states. Similarly, in the 1960s, the United States used guidelines on capital transfers by multinationals to strengthen its international monetary position. It has also been alleged that the United States government has on occasion been able to use, wittingly and unwittingly, the information-gathering capacities of global corporations domiciled in America for intelligence purposes.

Examples of political problems arising from instrumental use are not hard to find. Of sixteen conflicts cited by Behrman as arising from corporate activities among the Atlantic nations in the mid-1960s, twelve involved the American Trading with the Enemy Act, one involved computer technology related to nuclear weapons, and three involved enforcement of U.N. sanctions. In none of these cases did a corporation directly or deliberately provoke or profit from the conflict. In the data assembled by Leyton-Brown on sixty-one public conflicts in Britain, Canada, and France arising as the result of the activities of multinational corporations, interstate conflicts arose primarily from extraterritoriality problems. In only two cases did a multinational enterprise seek the diplomatic support of its parent government.

Manipulation of transnational corporations, however, is an instrument available to the host as well as the home government. This is an aspect of politics to which the U.N. report gave little attention. The most dramatic recent example was the 1973 oil embargo. While the companies exerted some independence in diverting non-Arab oil to the Netherlands and the U.S., the Arab countries were able to obtain enough company compliance in regard to Arab oil to be able to promote their foreign policy objectives. Even a small country like the Philippines was able to use a threat to nationalize American corporations in the 1960s to induce the U.S. government to extend trade preferences. Canada, with a third of its corporations foreign-owned (58 percent by value in manufacturing), is sometimes cited as a victim of a home government's ability to manipulate its corporations. In my study of thirty-one conflicts between the U.S. and Canada that reached the Presidential level in the 1950s and 1960s, nine involved the activities of transnational corporations.[5] In five of the nine, corporations played an active lobbying role, but in four others, they were used (successfully) as instruments by governments—twice by the U.S. and twice by Canada. The Canadian government achieved its objectives by obtaining letters of intent from the auto companies in the case of the auto pact; and by obtaining de facto acceptance of jurisdiction from Humble Oil in the Arctic sovereignty issue. In general, Canada did no worse in government bargaining in cases involving foreign corporations than those in which corporations were not involved.

Multinational corporations have their own interests, and when they are pressed in different directions by different governments, they cannot automatically be expected to be hard bargainers on behalf of the home government's interests. Indeed one might argue that where host governments are relatively coherent and clearsighted in their objectives, they may often do better in the tripartite bargaining of home, host, and corporation than the home government does. The Soviet government, for example, is able to play off corporate competitors against each other, and the liberal Western governments are often poorly placed to coordinate corporate behavior or to insure that the home government's interests are adequately represented. Or to take an example of a non-Commu-

[5] J. S. Nye, "Transnational Relations and Interstate Conflicts: An Empirical Analysis," *International Organization*, Autumn, 1974.

nist government, in 1974 Kuwait was able to successfully press Gulf and BP to raise the price they paid for Kuwaiti oil despite the failure of an earlier public auction and the expressed displeasure of the U.S. government.

Fixed investments can be hostages as well as outposts, and not only for governments. While force may be less applicable for some states, it is readily available to non-state groups. The corporation as hostage has provided a valuable instrument to non-state groups, both as a source of finance and as a means of destroying a government's credibility. For example, guerrillas in Argentina in the past year kidnapped twelve foreign officials and raised some 36 million dollars in ransom through the use of force against multinational corporations.

Force is not always necessary. The important point is that direct investment creates a transnational interdependence which various groups or governments may try to manipulate for their own political purposes. While the U.N. report seems to deplore this at some points, it is open to criticism for using a dual standard when it also invites home governments to influence corporations for positive social objectives in other countries.

INDIRECT ROLE: SETTING THE AGENDA

Why some issues rather than others absorb the attention of statesmen is a question of considerable political importance that has received too little attention. Even if they played no other role, the effect of multinational corporations in helping to set the agendas of interstate politics has been significant. Multinational corporations have affected the agenda of interstate relations both intentionally and unintentionally. The intentional effect on the agenda by lobbying for a particular policy of their home government toward the host country is familiar but nonetheless important. Such policies have sometimes taken the form of home government interventions in support of claims against host governments. For example, in the 1960s the dispute between the International Petroleum Corporation and the local government became a tail that wagged the dog of American policy toward Peru. In other cases, such as lobbying of

Congress by executives of multinational corporations in favor of more liberal tariff treatment of the host country by the home country, the lines of policy influence run in the other direction. Canada has benefitted from such allies in a number of instances. Perhaps most intriguing in light of supposed ideological differences has been the recent lobbying by business executives on behalf of more liberal trade arrangements with the Soviet Union. Nor is there much evidence for the charge that multinational corporations form a powerful lobby for a militaristic foreign policy. With a few exceptions, multinational (as distinct from merely large) corporations do not have a particularly strong stake in military-oriented production or activities.

This is not to argue that multinational corporations do not create conflicts among states, but that they have more often done so unintentionally than intentionally. Multinational corporations have had three major unintended effects on the political agenda. First, in the past decade, the transnational activities of such corporations have given rise to conflicts of jurisdiction and problems of extraterritoriality in such matters as antitrust, capital controls, trade restrictions, and taxation policies, as mentioned above.

Second, multinational corporations have affected the interstate agenda through their effects on transnational economic systems, particularly trade and money. Production by subsidiaries of corporations outside their home country has grown to over twice the value of trade among the developed countries. Moreover, a significant portion (more than a quarter of U.S. exports by some estimates) of international trade has been transformed from "arms length" to intra-enterprise transactions. The result is that a variety of new trade policy questions have been put on the intergovernmental agenda and they have become intertwined with a broader range of industrial policy questions. Similarly, the ability of a few score corporate treasurers, thinking globally and acting rationally, to transfer vast sums with extraordinary rapidity was one of the factors that contributed to the inability of countries to maintain an international monetary system based on fixed exchange rates.

Third, multinational corporations have unintentionally affected the agenda of interstate relations by stimulating other social groups to press for particular governmental policies. Some groups such as banks, advertising agencies, and some labor unions have been stimulated to press for policies of liberalization that permit them to emulate the transnational strategy of the multinational corporation. Other groups which are less transnationally mobile and feel themselves threatened or disadvantaged by the activities of the corporations have pressed their governments for protective or nationalist policies which subsequently burden the interstate agenda. The recent struggle between transnationally mobile corporations and the relatively immobile labor unions over the Burke-Hartke bill affecting the trade and investment policies of the United States is an apt example.

Long-term Effects on World Order

It is easier to identify the roles of multinational corporations in day-to-day processes of world politics than to assess their likely long-term effects on the structure of world politics. Will they become more important as actors or instruments in world politics or have they passed their period of prime political importance? If they continue or grow in importance, will they have beneficial or malign effects on the creation of a peaceful and just world order? Will they redistribute power, wealth, and status or lead to increasing concentration? Obviously there can be no clear answers to the questions, but it is equally obvious that the questions are too important to ignore. We can at least speculate about the prospects.

It is possible that the political importance of the multinational corporation is a product of a unique confluence of factors in world politics in the decades following World War II. A major aspect of this situation was American military strength and a geographically broad definition of security that resulted in what has been called a Pax Americana.

It is sometimes argued that the multinational corporation is largely a creature of American political preponderance in the period following World War II, and will recede in economic and political importance as the American government defines its security interest in less expansive terms in the aftermath of Vietnam. While there is certainly some relationship between the Pax Americana and the transnational activity of multinational corporations, it is not as simple as this "military-security determinism" implies. First, it is sometimes forgotten that the American multinational corporation arose in the nineteenth century when the United States was a net debtor; was *not* located primarily in the Caribbean and Latin America; and had already created fear of a *défi américain* in Europe at the turn of the century. American direct foreign investment was as large a percentage of GNP (7 percent) in 1914 as in 1966.

Second, the causes of growth and the causes of continued existence are not necessarily the same. Sorcerers' apprentices have been known to take on lives of their own. While the United States was the primary source of the rapid growth of multinational corporations in the postwar period, there is a current trend toward the development of European and Japanese-based multinationals. The preponderant American source (some 60 percent of book value of direct foreign investment in the mid-1960s) is slowly being eroded by the more rapid growth rates of European and Japanese direct investment. Moreover, the past and future relations of Swiss and Swedish multinationals to a Pax Americana is at best uncertain and indirect.

Third, some 70 percent of U.S. direct investment is located in other advanced industrial societies, not in the less developed countries, yet it is the latter which are the most likely areas to be left out of a more narrowly defined conception of national military security. In other words, the erosion of bipolarity and the decline of American hegemony need not diminish the role of multinational corporations, unless it were accompanied by a shift toward greater use of force and away from economic welfare goals. While it is true that multinational corporations exist within, and are affected by the structure of political-military relations in world politics, it does not follow that the postwar Pax Americana is the only such structure under which they could prosper.

A somewhat different case for projecting a decline in the political importance of multinational corporations might be based on long-term trends toward government intervention in economic affairs and the continued importance of nationalism. Neo-mercantilism is not a temporary aberration. Governments are unlikely to give free rein to organizations that powerfully affect their economies, and that threaten feelings of national autonomy and national status. The trend toward politicization of issues of direct foreign investment is likely to continue. Indeed, the process is prompted by the rapid growth and large scale of multinational corporations as they stimulate domestic groups to emulation and opposition.

Such politicization, however, need not imply a decline in political importance. If multinational corporations were merely a nuisance or an inconvenience, states could simply curtail them by resorting to restrictive economic policies or their police powers. Multinationals, however, present opportunities as well as problems. Governments are faced with trade-offs between their objectives of welfare and autonomy. Even when government controls constrain and diminish the direct corporate role in world politics, they may simultaneously increase the indirect importance of multinational corporations as an instrument or agenda item in intergovernmental politics.

The opposite projection, that multinational corporations will grow in importance in world politics, is sometimes based on the economic power expected to derive from gargantuan size. This argument is not compelling. Predictions that three hundred giant corporations will run the world economy tend to be based on simple projections of past 10 percent annual growth rates, and fail to take into account some of the disadvantages that appear with large size, particularly in manufacturing when temporary monopoly advantages conferred by a new technology have been competed away. Even smaller multinationals, however, can make crucial allocative decisions that challenge governments' welfare goals. The challenge to governments lies in global scope and mobility more than in corporate size. Corporate mobility (which is greater in service and some manufacturing than in extractive industries) is not only a challenge to small states, but also to large states like the U.S. (and particularly to groups like labor which influence the foreign policy of large states). If there is increased movement of some corporate headquarters and major divisions, whether to remote and pleasant tropical islands as some foresee, or simply in the form of shopping among developed states, the process of differentiating corporate and home government interests will be speeded along.

Most multinational corporations in the world today can be identified with a home country. They are multinational in operation, but rarely in ownership or top staff. Home governments tend to have jurisdiction over a major portion of the corporate empire's assets, and to have close informal ties with top management. Nonetheless, multinationality of operations can make a significant political difference. Corporate profits and growth come to depend on economic and political conditions in political jurisdictions other than that of their home government. Corporations gradually develop a view of their short-term interests coinciding with different governments at different times, and of their long-term interests as different from the interests of any particular state. The point was put rather dramatically by Carl Gerstacker, chairman of Dow Chemical, when he admitted to dreaming of buying a neutral island for Dow's headquarters, "beholden to no nation or society." The trend of corporate differentiation from home and host countries, has not yet gone very far. Of some 193 manufacturing firms that operate transnationally and for which data were available, the U.N. Secretariat found only 9 percent had more than 50 percent foreign content in employment; 7 percent derived half or more of their earnings from abroad; and some 14 percent had half or more of their sales abroad. Nonetheless, some corporate developments seem to point toward increased multinationality and autonomy of staff. Technological improvements are continuing to reduce the costs of communications and enhance the corporate capacity to develop global strategies divorced from identification with the interests of any particular country.

This trend is complemented, and to some extent reinforced, by the growing differentiation of political attitudes toward multinational corporations at home. A decade or more ago, multinationals were much less an object of domestic controversy, and it was widely assumed that the interests of American-based multinationals were roughly similar to the "national interest." Today the range of domestic attitudes is more diverse. The AFL-CIO has called for limits on direct foreign investment, and Senator Jackson has accused oil companies of disloyalty for obeying the government of Saudi Arabia and failing to sell Arab oil to the U.S. Navy. It is possible that such attitudes may force some firms to a closer identification with their home government, but it is equally likely that such attitudes will encourage other firms to further differentiate themselves from their original "home" government's jurisdiction. It is said that some American based corporations with nearly half their operations abroad planned in the event of Congressional passage of the Burke-Hartke legislation to establish binational structures with European headquarters handling operations outside the United States.[6]

Another facet of the growing differentiation of political attitudes toward multinational corporations is the diverse responses to incoming investments into the United States, which grew by over 10 percent per year in the early 1970s. Initial American responses not only to Arab but even to Canadian direct investment included a certain xenophobic element. On the other hand, German, Japanese, and Swedish multinationals bring jobs and may affect that part of labor's opposition that is based on the belief that "multinationals export jobs." Diversity of attitudes is likely to increase.

Multinational Corporations and Less Developed Countries

This is the area which received greatest attention in the United Nations. As the International Chamber of Commerce correctly pointed out, the *Report of the Group of Eminent Persons* did not focus on the area where over two-thirds of direct investment is carried out, that is, among the developed countries. Nonetheless, from a world order viewpoint the focus of the Group was politically justified. Multinational corporations pose greater political problems for less developed countries, because of the difference in scale (General Motors' annual profits exceed the annual income of most African states), the sensitivity of post-colonial and geographically

---

[6] I am indebted to Howard Perlmutter of the Wharton School for this point.

peripheral states to situations of dependence, and the frequency of internal cleavages that make their polities both penetrable and fragile. Moreover, poor countries have generally found themselves as hosts, but rarely as homes of multinational corporations.

There has been no shortage of arguments recently about the economic costs and benefits of multinationals to less developed host countries. Proponents point out that multinationals are one of the engines for transferring technology and relocating industrial production from the richer to the poorer parts of the globe. They argue that transnational organization is necessary to overcome what for many states is the economic irrationality of narrowly bounded political sovereignty. Unlike portfolio investment, the contribution of the multinational corporation is not so much the movement of capital as the organization of capital, management, technology, and access to rich country markets into an economic package which is greater than the sum of its parts.

Critics, on the other hand, argue that the parts of the package are often obtainable separately, and that the costs of "packaging" are too great. Among the costs sometimes charged to the corporation are inappropriate technology, creation of inefficient oligopoly patterns in small national markets, discouragement of local entre-preneurship, erosion of local economic policy and controls, stimula-tion of inappropriate consumer tastes, and illegitimate meddling in the local political process.

Facts can be marshalled on both sides of the economic argument, and the facts vary from case to case. However, from a given country's point of view, a frequent flaw in the arguments of proponents and critics who focus on the system as a whole, is a failure to ask the crucial question: "What are the realistic alternatives in a given situation?" In some cases a critical factor such as advanced technology can be obtained by licensing; in other cases it may be unobtainable except as part of a corporate package. In some cases, access to markets is a simple matter; in other cases access to protected markets in rich countries might be impossible without the sales network or political clout of a multinational corporation within its home country.

Less developed countries can follow a wide range of strategies vis-à-vis multinational corporations. At the two extremes are the strategies of laissez-faire and complete exclusion. The benefits or costs of exclusion look somewhat different depending on whether one thinks of it as the "Chinese" or the "Burmese" example. Another approach is to let multinationals enter on generous terms and renegotiate these terms as the factors that the corporations bring in become less scarce. This situation of "let them in and squeeze them later" has characterized many raw material investments, where the terms of the original bargain tend to become politically obsolete over time. A quite different approach is the "high threshold." The Andean Group of countries, for example, permit entry only on quite stringent conditions (including eventual divestment), which are agreed to by the corporation at the outset. Other countries permit entry only if corporations agree to joint ventures with local capital or the local government. A further variant of this approach is to disassemble the package of direct investment and allow corporations entry on contractual terms to provide a specific service. These various strategies are discussed at some length in the U.N. report. A recurrent theme in the dissenting comments is the fear that restrictive strategies will discourage corporate investment in less developed countries and inhibit the beneficial relocation of industrial production in the Southern part of the globe. Each of these strategies promises different costs and benefits for different countries, and for different economic sectors at different times. No single strategy or legal regime is likely to satisfy all countries, or even the same country over time. This makes agreements on international legal regimes distasteful to many less developed countries.

As we saw above, multinational corporations can also follow a number of political strategies in their bargaining with host states: (1) they can appeal to their home governments for support; (2) they can use their economic power to participate in the local political process, legally or illegally; and (3) they can organize external boycotts and restrictions of credit. Alternatively, the corporations can follow a fourth strategy. They can restrict themselves to economic agreements, attempt to convince host states that the corporation continues to bring in resources such as technology, market information, or management from which there is a joint gain. In other words, they can seek to prove that the goose roasted is worth less than the goose laying golden eggs. As Charles Robinson, president of Marcona Corporation has put it, "the only thing that counts is whether you are worth more alive than dead." If one is concerned with an international order that involves global equity and freedom of choice, it is the last of these, the "golden egg strategy," which is clearly preferable, and one which a U.N. commission charged with developing international codes of conduct should attempt to promote.

If the benefits of multinational corporations are as great as proponents claim they are then there should be no objection to letting host countries choose freely. If the economic, social, and political costs are as great as the critics charge, then host countries should be free to try to disassemble the package of direct investment and reject the transnational organization. But it is essential that the bargains be freely struck. Free choices require meaningful alternatives and accurate information. The task for international institutions would be to help enhance such opportunities for free political choice on such matters as how much aggregate growth a people are willing to sacrifice for autonomy and experimentation (and vice versa). This requires dispelling the fear and mistrust that frequently blocks clear appraisal of self-interest by poor, weak countries. It also means discouraging the use of home government influence that goes much beyond normal diplomatic representation, and discouraging corporate meddling in the political processes of the host state. As a number of comments in the U.N. report indicate, it is unrealistic to expect governments to refrain completely from support of their corporations. Nonetheless, the basic diplomatic norms should reflect the principle of free choice.

It is sometimes suggested that the only international institutions needed are those which would establish a legal order to facilitate the corporation's work. This view, however, fails to take into account the political roles of the corporation that we have described above. Even while they follow their economic pursuits, multinational corporations become involved in a political process which is too untidy and changeable to contain within a static legal order.

However, there are important political roles for international institutions in helping to increase joint gains in economic welfare and intelligent choices between welfare and other values.

Viewed from this perspective, the three major recommendations of the U.N. report do not appear as minimal as at first glance. Given deep-seated differences among countries, it was unrealistic to expect a strong supranational organization to oversee the activities of multinationals, or to expect agreement on George Ball's idea of global chartering of corporations or Charles Kindleberger's and Paul Goldberg's "GATT for direct investment." A global charter would formally denationalize corporate origin, but would remove none of the real conflicts stemming from the central dilemma of differing decision domains. As for a specific legal convention, the broader the agreement in numbers of countries or scope of subject matter, the less likely the prospects for success. The problem is not only one of organizing collective action among large numbers of states. It also stems from the basic political reality that underlies corporation-state bargaining, particularly between rich and poor. When the basic bargain is political and may be obsolescing over time, poor countries consider it unwise to institutionalize a set of norms or adjudication procedures that represent a stage in which they are relatively less favored.[7]

In other words, the recommendation of the creation of an expert commission charged with the task of continuing discussion and negotiation of codes of conduct is a more realistic approach to the task of creating and adjudicating norms than the more elegant solutions would be. As L. K. Jha, former Governor of the Bank of India and Chairman of the Group commented in the report, developing countries need not feel disappointed with the recommendation if they look upon the report as the beginning rather than the end of an exercise in the creation of norms.

In addition, the recommendations of creation of an information gathering and technical assistance capacity in the Secretariat are potentially of considerable importance. In the words of J. Irwin Miller, "the importance of information and disclosure can be

---

[7] On obsolescing bargains, see Raymond Vernon, *Sovereignty at Bay* (New York, 1971).

missed . . . [and] technical assistance is a promising adjunct to the work of the information center."

Differential access to information, variable identity, and mobility of resources are key assets of multinational corporations in their bargaining with states. Information that improves governments' information about global corporate activities and governments' knowledge about mutual alternatives can affect the terms of the bargain. Much of the information will be difficult to obtain and equally difficult to assess. Since knowledge is power, it will not be easily parted with, either by corporations or by governments. Many countries have weak rules for disclosure of corporate information, and sometimes governments find it in their advantage, on tax incentives for example, not to disclose the information they have. Even the Commission of the European Community, for example, has had to compile inadequate data on corporate mergers from public sources because some member governments refused to share the information that they collected nationally.

Nonetheless, the collation and sharing of information from public sources can be useful to many governments. Moreover, the amount of information in the public domain may increase as national demands grow for corporations to demonstrate their contribution to the local economy. Comparison of such company national reports by an international staff can identify discrepancies and raise important questions. The usefulness of the international institution will be greater the more the staff develops a reputation for fair-mindedness. This last point is essential, since the main sanction which a U.N. Commission on Multinationals would have is publicity. This is not an insignificant sanction against corporations dealing with the public, but it would be quickly dissipated by biased work.

Not all governments have the ability to make full use of the information already available to them. Providing experts in this area can be an important function. Technical assistance cannot remove all conflicts from the interaction of weak states and foreign corporations, but at least it can help to dispel the mistrust that stems from fear of the unknown, and allow the parties to bargain on the basis of more clearly perceived self-interest. The experience of

Harvard's Development Advisory Service in helping countries such as Liberia and Indonesia to improve the terms of their contracts with foreign corporations is an instructive example. Again, while controversy cannot (and should not) be completely avoided, a reputation for fair-mindedness is essential.

What are the prospects for the United Nations being able to play a constructive role? There are two sorts of obstacles. Specifically, there are the problems and pitfalls of "geographic distribution," extraneous politicization, and occasional bias that beset the U.N. system. Steering clear of the obstacles will be essential if a U.N. commission is to help smooth the difficult political relations between rich home countries, multinational corporations, and poor host countries.

Multinational Corporations and Developed Countries

The problems posed by multinational corporations for developed countries, particularly the large economies, do not, at first glance, appear to pose as serious questions for world order. Differences in scale are not as severe as they are in the case of poor countries. Societies are less fragile and less easily disrupted by the direct effects of a corporation's activities. However, while there are fewer problems arising out of the direct political role of multinationals than is true of poor (or small) countries, corporations have, as indicated earlier, important political effects on the agenda of interstate relations, and as instruments in interstate bargaining. The problems arise less out of the direct political role of corporations than out of the ways in which they increase interdependence among states.

The dangers for world order arise out of the temptations of governments (or social groups pressing governments) to manipulate this interdependence to ensure a greater share of the gains that are created by corporate investment. Uncoordinated tax incentives are a familiar example, but serious problems are also arising out of host governments' insistence on employment, research, or balance of payments effects which appear to threaten the welfare of the home government (or important groups in the home society). The danger to world order lies in possible retaliation and competition restrictions on corporate investment that not only destroy any joint gains, but may result in joint losses.[8]

The critical institutional point is whether countries resort only to unilateral efforts to cope with the policy interdependence which the corporations have created, or whether they perceive the importance of coordinated responses to their increased policy interdependence. One such effort is a code of conduct for corporations. Codes of conduct sometimes have an effect in terms of strengthening the hands of weaker governments. In 1966 when the United States government tried to press voluntary guidelines on corporations in Canada and elsewhere, the Canadian government responded with a Code of Conduct of good business behavior. Litvak, Maule, and Robinson in the book *Dual Loyalty* found that this code did have some marginal effects. Corporations were made somewhat more aware of sensitive political problems. Ideally, what is needed to ensure beneficial effects on world order among the developed states is not so much a code of conduct for corporations as a code of conduct for governments in responding to the problems of interdependence that corporations have created. Such codes of conduct for government imply a global industrial strategy. Efforts to achieve such codes through the Organization for Economic Cooperation and Development have thus far not been impressive.

Suggestions have been made, from time to time, for the creation of globally chartered corporations. As noted above, a global charter would formally denationalize corporate origin but would remove none of the real conflicts stemming from the central dilemma of differing decision domains between corporations and governments or problems arising from conflicting objectives of governments. On the other hand, there have been suggestions of an intergovernmentally-owned enterprise to exploit common resources such as the seabed or to develop areas of high technology. The crucial question is where the seat of management strategy would be within such a corporation. The experience of many intergovernmental ventures in

---

[8] See C. Fred Bergsten, "Coming Investment Wars?" *Foreign Affairs*, October 1974.

high technology have not been encouraging because political criteria have interfered with management.[9] Perhaps a more fruitful avenue would be to explore forms of joint ventures between private multinational enterprises able to provide flexible management strategies and an intergovernmental corporation that would set the broad political parameters within which the management strategies would operate.

One cannot be too optimistic about states reaching agreement on international codes or institutions or new types of corporations in the short run, because states have conflicting as well as complementary objectives. Governments are concerned about status as well as welfare, and they are sensitive about the disparities of national and nationally based corporate sizes. Moreover, governments and social groups will continue to use corporations as instruments to influence other states or social groups. Even where corporations have no national identity and are independent actors, some states may feel that they are net gainers compared to other states. It will be some time before governments of even the advanced industrial societies are prepared to develop a coherent international industrial policy.

On the other hand, there are several trends that increase the elements of common challenge which multinational corporations present to governments. One is the diversification of national sources of direct investment with a possible result that more of the crucial governments will feel the divided interest of being both home and host rather than merely home to multinational corporations. Second, there are trends within corporations toward differentiation of corporate interests from the interests of either their home or host countries. Third, there is the process of politicization which both reflects and stimulates the differentiation of domestic interests vis-à-vis corporations in home countries and provokes demands for increased governmental controls. The first response to these challenges is likely to be unilateral national efforts, rather than international cooperation. But conflicting unilateral policies can be self-defeating unless there are some international rules and mechanisms for coordination. Moreover, multinational corporations may

---

[9] M. S. Hochmuth, *Organizing the Transnational* (New York, Humanities, 1974).

find themselves so hindered by contradictory national regulations that they may press their home governments to initiate efforts to achieve greater international uniformity. At this point the prospects for international economic organization improve, whether it be the OECD, the U.N. or in new institutions. The task for statesmen is to be aware of both the economic and political effects of multinational corporations on the prospects for creating a better world order.

The political significance of the multinational company has been distorted by careless terminology. Thus those companies have been occasionally referred to as superpowers—as though they existed without accountability to governments. Mr. Seymour J. Rubin examines that myth in the following section of the chapter.

G. W. B.

S. J. R.: The Multinational Company as a Superpower

The issue of the multinational enterprise as either the instrument or the determinant of "home" state policy has been much controverted. Equally, that type of multinational which, because it is not constrained by its need either for resources—such as extractive and scarce materials—or for markets for its products, actual or contemplated, poses a problem for the economic and possibly political policies of home and host nation alike.

A number of commentators, some hostile, some approving, have suggested that there exists, or is on the way to creation, a sort of supranational corporation. Such an enterprise would presumably pursue its own interest, responsive, within the limits of its considerable power, to the nationalistic claims of neither home nor host. The objective fact is the growth of the size and the operations of multinational enterprise. The conclusions drawn from that fact vary widely. What seems to be the common assumption is that, as Samuel Pisar has put it, "multinational firms have detached

themselves from their American moorings and have taken off on the
high seas. Now they are stateless. . . ." Or, in the words of George
Ball, "The nation-state is no longer an adequate or even a very
relevant economic unit." Or, as an eminent scholar in the field,
Raymond Vernon, suggests, sovereignty is "at bay."

As suggested at the outset of this essay, the rise of the multinational and the asserted concomitant decline of the nation-state may
excite contradictory sentiments. Even without considering the
broad philosophical implications of internationalization of world
business, differences may arise as to the merit of relatively minor
manifestations of internationalization. A policy of using non-Ameri-
can nationals as executives of an American-based multinational is
as appealing to host nations as it may be distasteful to American
labor. The effort to be impartial, to be the instrument of neither
home nor host nation, to do what business presumably can do
best—that is, produce and distribute efficiently—runs into the
opposition of those who conceive such a concept, given the extent of
the multinational holdings and activities, as a threat to national
independence. Curious contradictions arise: thus, the disapproving
citation of the chairman of a British subsidiary of an American
parent that such an executive "must set aside any nationalistic
attitudes and appreciate that in the last resort his loyalty must be to
the shareholders of the parent company and he must protect their
interests . . ." even as against the interests of the host nation,
appears, not in an attack by host nations, but in a statement
prepared by the AFL-CIO.

Examining these issues from the viewpoint of multinational-home
nation relations, one encounters attitudes which find curiously
small reflection in the various international studies of the multinational which have characterized the 1970s. Perhaps it is the fact
that the definition of the problem determines the outcome; but the
report of the United Nations Group of Eminent Persons focuses
almost exclusively on conflict with host—not home—states. In the
statement of such issues as "The exercise of direct control over the
allocation of one country's resources by residents of another . . ."
the report obviously deals exclusively with such worries as those of
the Andean group, not with the concerns, for example, of American

or British labor about export of jobs. It is of course the fact that the
U.N. report centers on development; but even there the possibility
that the multinational may clash with its home as well as with its
host state receives little if any mention. The home nation of most
multinationals remains the United States; and there the ability of
the multinational to transcend "nationalistic" concerns appears in
a context quite other than that of the studies sponsored by the
United Nations, or the U.N. Conference on Trade and Develop
ment, or the Meeting of Foreign Ministers of the American
Republics.

Yet the most important of the home nations, the United States,
has seen a vast increase in demands for not only protection from
foreign imports but restriction on the American-based multinational's vaunted freedom of decision. The proposals put before the
Congress by Messrs. Burke and Hartke, while unlikely to be
enacted in anything like their original form, furnish a fair catalogue
of the asserted evils which the multinational visits on the home, not
the host, nation. Where the host has traditionally complained that
the ability of the multinational to establish transfer prices results in
a drain of resources from host nations in which subsidiaries are
located, the argument is made that, in the interest of minimizing
taxes, American multinationals have sought in fact to maximize
profits abroad, not at home. Thus, there is now more activity than
ever before under Section 482 of the Internal Revenue Code, which
permits the Commissioner of Internal Revenue to reconstruct prices
used in intra-enterprise transfers, so as to allocate for tax purposes a
fair share of the profits to the United States. The traditional
argument in the international forum has been that the multinational, in time of business difficulty, closes down the plant in the
host and keeps that in the home nation functioning; the contention
now is that the multinationals are exporting jobs, that they prefer
the cheaper labor markets abroad to the more costly ones at home,
that they establish "sister plants" abroad for the purpose of shifting
production there even when the product is re-imported back into
the United States, and that their export of technology as well as of
production is turning the United States into a service economy—a
nation of hamburger stands.

Answers abound to the charge that "American-based multinational firms export American jobs, export American technology, and export American capital." Indeed, the participant in an international discussion is more likely to hear that the American-based multinational is an octopus feeding on the host nations to the benefit of the American economy. And such impartial statistics as are available and understandable seem to indicate that American-based multinationals have done better by the American economy than have entirely domestic companies. It is argued that the multinationals which account for the major share of foreign direct investment produce the preponderant share of the U.S. trade surplus in manufactured items; that these companies are in the most rapidly growing industries domestically; and that their international investment pays large dividends not only in domestic sales and investment, but also in employment.

In this controversy, is it the essential fact that the multinationals are indeed the creatures of neither home nor host, and that they pursue their own objectives independent of the feeble controls sought to be imposed upon them by either state? Have they in fact relegated the nation-state to a position of subservience? Are they really supranational entities, in their actions and their power, even if the corporate headquarters continues to be Wilmington?

The answer would seem to be that these questions are incapable of direct reply. To a certain extent, a business enterprise which stretches across national boundaries has capacities which are beyond those of the purely domestic company. Some of these capacities are the simple functions of the economies of scale; some result from a more advantageous relation to supplies, power, workers, and markets; some result from the ability of such an enterprise to shift resources as circumstances warrant, to make themselves a major share of the decisions as to how much taxes they should pay, in what time period, and where, to hedge by currency transfers or by leads and lags against the devaluation of one currency or the expected appreciation of another. Such a firm has choices available to it, many of which may prejudice national policies of one or another of the nation-states in which the multinational operates.

This, however, is far from a statement that the nation-state is powerless—any more than it is in dealing with its own mammoth corporate entities. It is suggested that General Motors, by virtue of its size, may determine American economic policy to a degree not immeasurably less than does the Government; but this has been a commonplace of economic thought at least since the early publications of Berle and Means. That prices may be "administered" hardly denies all authority to government. And, in many ways, governmental actions are reminding the multinationals that the nation-states have not as yet been brought to their knees.

The legal methods of these reminders are various. In the United States, Congressional inquiries, as well as public concern for what seem to be extraordinary profits for some multinationals at a time of general economic difficulty, have led to several suggestions of controls. The increased use of Section 482 of the Internal Revenue Code has been mentioned. Tax legislative experts are contemplating reforms in the basic tax structure, which have enabled multinationals to treat foreign taxes paid as credits against American taxes due. Inquiry is being made into the allocation for tax purposes of expenses for research and development, with the thought that some portion of such expenses ought to be allocated to foreign activities. American firms which have used the "sister plant" concept are visibly worried by the attacks on the present ability to re-import components to the United States against payment of duty only on the value added abroad. A hitherto obscure section of the Internal Revenue Code, Section 807 of the United States Tariff Schedule, has become a battleground.

That the multinational has a considerable ability to transcend the limitations of home nation policy is reasonably clear. Tariff walls—on both sides—have been surmounted, through local production, or through devices like Tariff Schedule Section 807. Labor markets have been integrated, the case of United States and Canadian automobile unions comes to mind. Capital markets, which governments may desire to keep separate, are linked not only by the original equity investment in a foreign subsidiary, but also by the intracompany transactions, and by the need to finance expansion, which has resulted in a substantial international bond market. Most disturbing to governments has been the participation by the multinationals in short-term capital transactions—the "sloshing" of corporate funds back and forth as corporate treasurers seek to beat the money game, and, probably as important, the less visible leads and lags in the handling of intracompany accounts.

It seems unlikely, however, that all of this adds up to superpower for the multinationals. At the very least, there are available counter measures, perhaps more available to the home than to the host nation. The suggestions for revisions of tax, antitrust, securities, even patent legislation, now under discussion in the United States indicate that the government has authority, if it chooses to wield it. Such collateral debatable but possibly effective measures as those proposed by Senator Adlai Stevenson, Jr., to set up a sort of TVA in the energy field to compete with the large integrated oil companies, and to establish a measure for both results and profits, indicates (the merits aside) what can be done. To the extent that a home nation chooses to cooperate with one or another of the suggestions for international regulation of the multinational, another constraint could be added.

It is not evident that substantial new general constraints are needed. Some of the abuses—the speculation in currencies which tends to defeat intergovernmental efforts in currencies which tends to defeat intergovernmental efforts toward stability—can and should be curbed. But it may well be that there are limits on the power and on the growth of the multinational which are operative, and which make the problems less than apocalyptic. One of these constraints is the likelihood that largeness is not necessarily the equivalent of efficiency. The large organization has efficiencies of scale; it also has the problems of management inherent in any large bureaucracy, the tendency of managers to take the safe rather than the possibly better decision, the ability, because of size and complexity and failures of intracompany communication, to hide mistakes which eventually bring about—as in the case of the Pennsylvania Railroad—a crash which might have been averted by earlier action. The possible analogy of the multinational to the dinosaur has been noted.

Limitations exist, too, on the much vaunted mobility of the

multinational. The nature of the business (the extractive industries have been mentioned) may impose its own constraints. Sales must be made where the customers are. There is an evident difficulty of moving physical plant from one location to another, and there is large investment in such a plant. Moreover, laws, in home or host nations, may inhibit corporate action. To shut down a plant may be as difficult as to open it. Assets of one subsidiary may be hostage, as in the case of Deltec in Argentina, for liabilities of another. And managers of subsidiaries, respectful of the communities in which they live and work, are likely to find that the interests of the host nation are in fact in close correspondence with those of the shareholders of the parent company.

Finally, it may be that the era of the rapid growth of multinationals—especially American-based multinationals—will not continue as before. Some projections seem to assume that the conditions of the modern world are such that multinationals will continue to increase their absolute and their relative share of world trade and industry. But that conventional wisdom may be questioned. A number of circumstances which favored the growth of the multinational have changed. Similarly, circumstances have altered in a manner which suggests that the problem issues may arise in a less aggravated form in the future than they have in the past.

Thus, one can speculate that the phenomenal rise of the American-based multinational was attributable, in the period after World War II, to the rapid expansion of the world economy at a time when capital, technology, and managerial skills were concentrated in the United States. Certainly the creation of the European Economic Community, with its common tariff, encouraged the enterprising Americans, more used to a philosophy of expansion than their European cartel-minded competitors, to leap from exports to Europe to production in Europe. Additionally, the Americans had the advantage of vast quantities of dollars, both at home and abroad, available at a rate of exchange which made acquisitions abroad an irresistible bargain. Not all of these factors were responsible for the expansion of the multinationals, and they do not necessarily relate to areas other than Europe (though they undoubtedly had an effect elsewhere as well). But this combination of circumstances is unlikely to recur. With changed circumstances, one can question whether it is appropriate to extrapolate the trend of the 1960s and early 1970s into a world dominated by giant (mostly American) multinationals.

Some of the problems seem likely to be less virulent than they have been. Floating exchange rates, for example, would seem to diminish the sloshing of corporate funds from one currency to another. The not entirely welcome attention focused everywhere, certainly in the United States, on the activities of multinationals and on their asserted conflict with or indifference to national policy can be counted on to affect the conduct of the multinationals. Internationalization of labor as well as industry, rates of inflation even higher abroad than in the United States, may well result—as in the Panasonic-Motorola situation—in Japanese industry coming to the United States—thus confusing the case of the American labor unions. The situation may be complicated, but it seems increasingly unlikely that the multinational will, in fact, be the master of nations.

Conclusion

New problems have been created as a result of the rise of the multinational, many of them relating to the use of the multinational by the home nation as a conduit for its policy, by the suspicion that the home nation is the faithful servant of the interests abroad of the multinational, or by the uncomfortable feeling that the multinational owes fealty to no sovereign and accompanies that independence with awesome power. The linkage of product and capital markets which has been accomplished with the assistance of the multinational, the flow of technology, the market for labor skills, have created benefits. But these aspects of the internationalization of production have also created or exacerbated difficulties. The more explicit aspects of some of these difficulties have been duly noted: the cases of asserted extraterritoriality, of use of governmental power to rescue the private foreign investment, of currency speculation in the face of international efforts to achieve stability. It seems likely that many of these instances are but the tip of the iceberg—that the unnoted effects of the multinational, perhaps particularly in its alliance with its home government, are more important than those which surface. Yet, because of changing economic and political circumstances, including the fierce light of publicity which has been brought to bear, the balance between sovereignty of nations and the power of multinationals is being, if it has not already been, restored.

This restoration of balance makes possible a realistic appraisal of what ought to be the relation between the United States—or any other home government—and its multinationals. There is some feeling that a too intimate relationship may be a burden on government and business alike—a recognition that there is not an inevitable correspondence between the interests of the United States and its national companies abroad. For many reasons, the United States has thus been reluctant to cut off aid to nations which have nationalized American investment, despite Congressional enactments which encourage such a course; the interests of the United States are seen as broader than those of the private investor; and the efficacy of the step is doubted. As this recognition that there may be divergent interests develops, the role of the multinational in the determination or the implementation of foreign policy may well diminish. A friendly but independent spirit would seem appropriate and beneficial. There are signs that this is developing.

Eugene Rostow, Joseph Nye, and George Ball

10

The Need for International Arrangements

A number of proposals have been made for giving legitimacy to the multinational company by bringing it under some kind of international or supranational regulation. Professor Eugene V. Rostow proposes a treaty for that purpose. Professor Joseph Nye foresees the need for "procedures, codes, and international institutions" that would help resolve the conflicts between corporations and nation-states. Mr. George W. Ball proposes an international charter as a possible solution in the years to come.

G. W. B.

E. V. R.: The Need for a Treaty

In 1968, the United Nations Conference on Trade and Development (UNCTAD) adopted a resolution which set in motion a long series of studies and discussions, first within UNCTAD, and then under the jurisdiction of the Economic and Social Council. Resolution 33 [II], March 28, responded to an American suggestion. Recognizing the important role that private foreign investment can play in the economic development of developing countries, and that a continuing dialogue between developed and developing countries is necessary in the interest of increasing the flow of private foreign investment to developing countries, it requested the Secretary General of the United Nations to undertake studies on the full range of problems involved in the process of private investment in developing countries, and to make recommendations for action "with a view to providing useful guidelines to both developed and developing countries."

The purpose of the American proposal at UNCTAD, the head of the American delegation to the Conference explained, was to make possible a rapid increase in the transfer of capital, entrepreneurship, and technology to the developing countries.

> We believe that one of the important achievements of this Conference could be to launch an inquiry into the legal and policy framework within which private investment and private entrepreneurship are drawn into the development process. Such an effort could make these indispensable factors of growth more readily available to the developing countries. Such a study might lead to widespread agreement on a fair code defining the rights and the obligations of foreign business enterprise in the developing countries—a balanced and agreed code, which could simplify and speed up the process of investment.

> We realize that this is a vast and many-sided subject and that some important progress in the field has been achieved in recent years. But my Government believes that much remains to be done and that the United Nations is the forum in which such an effort should be made.

> We have no desire to impose our own particular economic system on others. Every country, we recognize, must evolve its own economic system according to its own needs, its traditions, and the realities that it faces. But we do believe that the time has come for a new look at the problem as a whole. We believe that it should be possible through international agreement to bring about a basic improvement in the legal environment for private investment in the developing countries, which could quicken the flow of private resources into development.

In making this proposal, the American government hoped to achieve a multilateral treaty which would in effect become an international corporation law, capable of accomplishing for the world economy what modern corporation laws have accomplished for national economies. Under such a treaty, corporations could register without losing their nationality, and thereby acquire at least a *prima facie* right to do business in signatory countries; by registering, they would not only receive specified rights, but also accept correlative legal duties. The administration and enforcement of the treaty would be entrusted to a small international secretariat.

The American proposal fully recognized the legitimacy of widespread concerns, particularly in the developing countries, about the political and economic influence foreign corporations might acquire or exercise within the countries in which they did business. Its goal was a code of law to govern such activities in accordance with agreed principles, which should protect the interest both of the corporation and of the host countries.

Such a treaty could also fill an important gap in the existing international legal system. Many multinational companies, large and small, now operate without fully effective legal control over their financial and managerial affairs—the normal subject matter of corporate law. They are sometimes nearly beyond the reach of the law of the state of their domicile, and often beyond the reach of the law of the host state as well. These problems, which affect the functioning of many aspects of the international economy, can only be resolved by international agreement. Many complex issues of policy fall into this classification—the provision of remedies for fraud, the supervision of the Euromarket and other unregulated pools of funds, the control of monopolies and restrictive business practices, the transfer of technology and know-how. Issues of this kind are of as much concern to the industrialized nations as to the developing ones.

The 1968 UNCTAD resolution helped to stimulate a process of study and debate which included the Pearson Report in 1970, and, in 1974, the *Report of the Group of Eminent Persons on the Impact of Multinational Corporations on Development and on International Relations.* The contemplation of the problem by official bodies has been accompanied by a normal number of scholarly monographs on the subject.

The *Report of the Group of Eminent Persons* recommended the establishment of a Commission on Multinational Corporations under the supervision of the Economic and Social Council of the United Nations. The Commission, the report urges, should be regarded as the first step in a comprehensive program of study, discussion, negotiation, and practical action, intended to develop an appropriate combination of national and of international policies for governing multinational corporations. The report places primary emphasis on the improvement of national policies with regard to the role of multinational companies in facilitating growth and development, particularly within the developing nations. But it recognizes a need for the international coordination of national policies, and perhaps for international action as well. Therefore it recommends that the Commission

(d) Undertake work leading to the adoption of specific arrangements or agreements in selected areas pertaining to activities of multinational corporations.

(e) Evolve a set of recommendations which, taken together, would represent a code of conduct for Governments and multinational corporations to be considered and adopted by the Council, and review in the light of experience the effective application and continuing applicability of such recommendations.

(f) Explore the possibility of concluding a general agreement on multinational corporations, enforceable by appropriate machinery, to which participating countries would adhere by means of an international treaty.

One of the eminent persons, the brilliant Swedish economist and banker Tore Browaldh, commented on the report in these terms:

A basic cause of the present concern with the impact of the multinational corporations is that nations are confronted by a radically new world, where international integration in the cultural and economic field continues at a very rapid pace, while Governments hang on to old policies that are increasingly divorced from reality. Many of the so called multinational corporation problems can be solved by appropriate national legislation or by Governments stating in the form of long-term development plans what their economic and social aims are and what they expect of those enterprises that operate within their borders. Other issues call for joint efforts and international collaboration on the part of Governments, who still are more apt to think in nationalistic terms.

The chief obstacle to the development of policies based on reality, Browaldh says, is the unwillingness of men and of governments to recognize developments which contradict their favorite political or ideological stereotypes.

Professor Joseph S. Nye, Jr., one of the ablest scholars working in the field, remains dubious about the possibility of tackling the bundle of problems associated with multinational companies by a treaty. He concludes that the treaty approach, which is supported

by George W. Ball, and by Professors Charles Kindleberger and
Paul Goldberg, as well as by the present writer, is too ambitious,
and politically utopian. "Given deep-seated differences among
countries," he writes, "it is unrealistic at this stage to expect, for
example, a strong supranational organization to oversee the
activities of multinationals, or the global chartering of corporations." It is preferable, he says, to continue to rely on the process of
individual bargaining and negotiation, case by case, between the
multinational company and the host country. It will become
politically possible to talk about multilateral international arrangements, Nye contends, only when the existing pattern of practice
becomes hopelessly cumbersome and expensive, through the multi-
plication of contradictory national policies and regulations.

We cannot afford to indulge in the many luxuries of the cynical
rule that things will have to get worse before they can be expected
to get better. I continue to believe that only the treaty approach
could begin to meet the necessities of the present situation, at least
for the developing nations. There is no shortage of capital in or
among the industrialized countries. Most of the activities of
multinational companies, save for the production of minerals and
other raw materials, are directed to the industrialized sector of the
international economy. The situation is different for the developing
nations. Their problem is that the existing procedures of case-by-
case bargaining between the company and the host country are not
capable of meeting the magnitude of the challenge they face. They
are too slow and too costly—and too often marred by corruption.
They simply cannot permit the mobilization of a large enough flow
of capital and entrepreneurship to the developing nations—a flow,
that is, large enough, and diverse enough, to achieve the full
utilization of the manpower of those countries, and their potential
for growth. There are exceptions, of course—Taiwan, for example,
and a few other countries whose law is hospitable to international
enterprise. But the general rule holds.

Professor Nye and others contend that political sensitivities make
it impossible to expect a treaty of this kind to be ratified soon by
more than a handful of developing countries. I should reply that
such a result would be preferable to abandoning or postponing the

effort altogether, and leaving the problem to chance, and bilateral bargaining alone. Even if an international treaty were accepted in the first instance by only a few developing nations, others could be expected to sign if experience under the treaty turned out to be favorable.

Under the best of circumstances, it would take many years to achieve a system of international legal arrangements capable of guiding and controlling the international economy, and organizing a flow of capital adequate to its needs. The pace of change in economic life regularly outstrips the efforts of governments even to anticipate what will happen next, to say nothing of the far more difficult task of controlling it. In the nature of the problem, we cannot afford another decade or two of delay, until the situation becomes dangerous enough to make political action possible.

J. S. N.: Two Views of World Order

If the trends toward growth and differentiation of multinational corporate interests from national interests continue, would the effect on world order be benign or malign? Not surprisingly, there is a good genie and a bad genie theory of whatever may be escaping from the national bottles.

The optimistic view sees the growth of multinational corporate autonomy as having a profound potential for transforming world politics and creating a better world order. As corporations grow in autonomy, they will transform world politics from a contest among states into a broader game with more actors who focus on primarily welfare oriented goals. Multinational corporations will become a vehicle by which mankind transcends the nation-state, our dominant international institution of the past four centuries. States will not cease to exist, but transnational production units will replace a large part of their role in providing citizen's welfare and will claim a proportionate share of their loyalties. These broadened economic domains will call forth new political institutions that go beyond the nation-state.

The optimists see the multinational corporation tying the world together in a meaningful way. It shifts industrial production toward the poorer parts of the globe. It transfers technology and managerial resources from advanced to less developed countries. It promotes both regional and global economic integration. *The Economist* of London has predicted, for example, that by the end of the century, most automobile and machinery production will be carried out in less developed countries. As it becomes politically difficult to bring workers from poor countries to jobs in rich countries, multinational corporations will promote global economic integration by taking the jobs to the workers.

The multinational corporation may also help to erode the great ideological cleavage that divides the world. Already there are more than one thousand agreements between Western corporations and Communist countries. Many of these are simple arrangements for "turnkey" plants. A multinational corporation builds a plant, turns it over to the Communist government, and is paid out of future production. But a number of Communist countries in Eastern Europe have found that longer term managerial involvement by the multinational corporation is a better way to insure continuous inputs of managerial and technological resources. Now some Eastern European governments have followed this logic a step further and have invested abroad, often in joint ventures with multinationals. Such decisions reflect the view that high growth rates depend on access to world markets and the latest generation of technology. The only way to insure access to both is not merely to be a host country, but to participate fully in the global information systems that provide multinational corporations with many of their advantages. Should this trend continue, it would require ideologists to reinterpret their view of imperialism as the transfer of labor's surplus value across national borders and raise questions about simple equations of multinational corporations, capitalism, and imperialism.

Looking further ahead toward the end of the century, it is possible that the multinational corporation will itself evolve into a new and flexible form of functional international organization. Not only will Eastern European governments participate, but with increasing politicization of the question of control of multinationals in their former home countries, demands may increase for government, labor, or consumer group representation on their management boards. Large segments of world industrial production will be managed by large public and quasi-public multinational corporations as well as a host of smaller private ones. Autonomous management (regardless of ownership) will provide flexibility and efficiency in the organization of global production. Questions of public vs. private ownership will have been transcended. Only questions of managerial autonomy vs. democratic control will remain.

Pessimists share with optimists many of these projections of the future of the corporations, but they see the malign effects prevailing over the benign. The economic benefits of global integration will be unevenly spread and some areas will gain very little. The resulting inequality is likely to breed conflict. Moreover, even if multinational corporations distribute industrial production more evenly about the globe than is now the case, they will tend to centralize strategic decisions in regional coordinating centers and at global corporate headquarters. As Stephen Hymer put it, high level decision-making about what technologies and which areas to develop will be taken in a few key cities in the advanced countries, surrounded by regional sub-capitals, while the rest of the world will be confined "to lower levels of activity and income, *i.e.* to the status of towns and villages in a new Imperial System." This might not matter if economic welfare were the only goal that people seek. But middle classes seek high status occupations that are associated with managerial and research functions. In addition, people often desire status for their nations, and some sense of autonomy, of helping to shape decisions rather than always feeling shaped by them. Such people fear that the transnational systems of production organized by multinational corporations will perpetrate and even accentuate an international economic structure that leaves them dependent on the advanced countries. Slogans of "global interdependence" frequently gloss over the reality that it makes an important political difference if one party is continually more dependent than the other.

As multinational corporations become more autonomous, this sense of dependence, threatened status, and lost autonomy may not be confined to poor countries. Social groups and regions within advanced countries may experience the same feelings. Autonomous corporations are a challenge to governments and politically important groups in large states as well as small. Rather than seeing this diminution of the role of the nation-state as a sign of healthy progress, pessimists see it as a new feudalism. Kings and corporate barons will engage in conflicts and coalitions, but the serfs of the world will suffer. The real global divisions will not be among nations, but between a world city knit together by transnational elites; and the diverse but intense parochialisms of the world countrysides. In the view of David Calleo and Benjamin Rowland, the decline of the nation-state would not be a sign of health, but a sign of disaster for "a sound international order cannot be built on the wreckage of nation-states." The nation-state provides the internal order and sense of political community that underlie democratic institutions. Our concept of democracy is closely intertwined with the concept of national community. Our political norms have not kept pace with the evolution of transnational corporate political roles.

Inevitable Conflicts and Joint Benefit Solutions

It is unlikely that there are any prognoses that represent reality as it will be at the end of the century. What is clear, however, is that there are important implications for current and future world order. Even if the three roles of multinational corporations in day-to-day political processes did not exist, these effects on the long-term structure of world politics are sufficient to justify the attention of a United Nations charged by its Charter to achieve cooperation and harmonization of the actions of nations.

Multinational corporations and nation-states are likely to coexist in an uneasy relationship of both conflict and cooperation. To a certain extent they are complementary institutions. With a few notorious exceptions, most corporations pursue a relatively specific set of economic objectives in comparison with the broad range of goals that characterize the territorial political community of the nation-state. Each institution can profit from the activities of the other.

But conflict is also endemic in the relationship. Multinational corporations present threats as well as benefits in terms of the broadened concept of national security that we outlined above. First, as nonterritorial entities without military force, corporations are not a threat to the physical survival of a nation, but their economic power can be used to threaten particular political parties or ruling regimes. Second, in relation to national autonomy multinational corporations may bring in the technological and managerial resources that enhance national autonomy vis-à-vis other states and vis-à-vis corporations in the long run, but there may be high costs in terms of autonomy in the short term and possibly over the long run as well if a structure of dependent relationships becomes firmly established with strong local roots. Third, in relation to status, corporate contributions to development may enhance status, vis-à-vis other states, but beyond a certain threshold foreign ownership, particularly if high status managerial and research jobs are concentrated abroad, may be seen as a threat to national status. This problem has become a concern of many Canadians over the past decade, and is reflected in the provisions of the new investment screening legislation.

Finally, even in regard to economic welfare, where corporate benefits are likely to be greatest, a certain amount of conflict is unavoidable. What distinguishes the modern multinational enterprise from the large international corporations of earlier centuries is its global management strategy made possible by the technology of modern communications. This means that the managers of multinational corporations are allocating resources within domains that cut across the national boundaries of both home and host countries. Therein lies an important potential for conflict. The most honest corporate manager acting rationally within a transnational perspective is bound to have conflicts of interest with the most reasonable of statesmen whose rationality (and democratic responsibility) is bounded by national frontiers. For example, Chrysler resisted British government pressures in 1971 and granted an inflationary wage increase to its British workers, not because it wished to thwart the government but because the increased wage costs were less important, from a global point of view, than avoiding disruption of production for the American small car market.

Given this complex pattern of potential threats and benefits that multinational corporations present in relation to a variety of national values, it is sensible to expect conflictual relationships. It is equally likely, however, that the conflicts will frequently be of the type that have solutions from which both parties can benefit. In many instances, the enlarged size of the pie can be more important than the size of the slices. A basic principle for an international economic order will be to enhance situations in which joint gains are perceived and shared by states and corporations. This will help to diminish the intensity of conflicts. However, since many national values are involved, and their intensity may vary among nations and over time, a second and equally important principle must underlie a just international economic order. National communities must be allowed to decide for themselves what degree of interdependence with corporations they find optimal, and what they are willing to pay for it.

In principle, at least, it should be possible to establish procedures, codes, and international institutions which help to insure that the inevitable conflicts have joint gain solutions and that multinational corporations have a positive effect on a peaceful and just world order. In practice, however, the solutions are not so simple. Part of the problem stems from misunderstanding and suspicion, but part stems from real differences of interests among governments. In analyzing the institutional questions it is useful to distinguish the problems of less developed countries from those that arise among the developed countries. While the latter are of greater economic importance, the former are of great political importance for world order.

G. W. B.: Proposal for an International Charter

In a characteristic spirit of pragmatism many American companies have attempted to work out their own compromises with national interests by trying to establish themselves as useful citizens of host countries, in the hope of mitigating the prejudices and fears they might otherwise engender. Most of their thinking has been in terms of protective coloring. Should they take local partners? Should they list the shares of their subsidiaries on local exchanges? Employ local managers? Try to behave as if the company's corporate children were national companies of host countries which only distantly acknowledged their absentee parents?

Such efforts to achieve a local identity should not, of course, be rejected out of hand, though clearly they are more suited to certain types of corporate activity than to others. Yet, in many cases, the cost of seeking recognition as a local citizen can be excessive. The peculiar genius of the multinational company stems from its ability to view the world economy from a single point of vantage and to deploy resources without regard to national origin in response to a common set of standards. It is the disadvantage of local partners that they are, in a sense, enemies of such mobility, since their judgments are based on benefits to the local subsidiary rather than on the interests of the world enterprise as a whole. Put another way, the scope of their thinking is defined by the national economy rather than the world economy.

This fundamental difference in attitude inevitably produces conflicts over corporate policy affecting a wide spectrum of issues that can be reconciled only through an accommodation of interests at some cost to the full efficiency of the multinational company. Such conflicts are, for example, likely to occur with respect to dividend policy. A local partner may wish earnings distributed, while the management of the multinational company may wish to plough them back—or vice versa. Or a local partner may wish particular facilities expanded, while the multinational company management finds it more profitable to sell or abandon them. Finally, the management of a world company may well find itself wishing to serve the market of a neighboring country, not by production in the host country but through subsidiaries located elsewhere.

To avoid such conflict we must find a more rational means of compromising the conflict between the multinational company and the host nation, yet that will require us to come to grips with the dubious legitimacy of the power of absentee corporate managements. Where does one find a legitimate base for the decisions of a corporate management that can profoundly affect the economic life of a nation to whose government it has only limited responsibility?

Ever since the publication in the early 1930s of Berle and Means' classic study of the divorcement of control from ownership in great industrial companies, Americans have puzzled over the problems of legitimacy in the domestic context. Whence do corporate managements (which are in practice frequently self-perpetuating) derive the right to make decisions affecting not only the inarticulate mass of shareholders, but the economic welfare of whole communities and the pocketbooks of consumers?

That question is far from simple even in domestic terms. When translated to the level of world operations, it acquires additional layers of complexity. Within our own national boundaries, an industrial corporation is made responsible not only to state authorities, but, in its larger operations, to regulatory agencies of the federal government. For a multinational company, however, the lack of an overriding political entity to oversee the totality of its operations is a major source of weakness.

Paralleling this deficiency is the fact that, if the nation-state cannot defend itself completely from the irresponsible exercise of power by the multinational company, the multinational company has no means for defending itself against the stultifying power of a host government that can destroy the efficiencies inherent in its multinational operations. In other words, there is no organic arrangement to prevent national governments from interfering with the company's activities in world commerce in the same way that the United States Constitution—enforced by the federal judiciary— limits the power of states to interfere with a domestic company's role in interstate commerce.

Not only is there a need for some ground rules to limit the

interference of host governments in the affairs of multinational corporations, but domiciliary governments should also be under some sensible constraint in employing multinational corporations to extend their jurisdictional reach into other countries. Thus, nothing is more abrasive in international relations than the efforts of one state to apply its laws extraterritorially in contravention of the laws and policies of another state; yet the United States has been one of the worst offenders, due in part to the overzealousness of the Washington bureaucracy and our idiosyncratic trade policies with regard to China and Cuba. On all too many occasions we have aggravated our deteriorating relations with Canada by trying to block Canadian subsidiaries of American companies from engaging in trade that the Canadian government was actively encouraging. Even today we are inviting resentment and retaliation by forbidding the Canadian subsidiary of an American firm to sell locomotives to Cuba or the Argentine subsidiary of a Detroit company to sell the Cubans trucks and automobiles. Finally, the continuing practice of applying our antitrust laws extraterritorially has goaded foreign governments to understandable outrage, even though, in that instance, the controlling fact is not American ownership of a company but the relation of its activities to American trade.

Over the past few years there have been several suggestions for codes of conduct to regulate foreign investment. But they have not made much progress, largely because they have been too broadly focused. Sooner or later we should forthrightly face the need for a better institutional mechanism to adjust the world's interest in efficient resource use through the multinational corporation with the local interest of nation-states. Such an adjustment should not prove beyond the wit of man. The experience of overlapping sovereignties is not new. The Roman Church, for example, coexisted with European dynasties for several centuries.

To some extent, the problem is complicated by the inadequacy of the forms and fictions in which the issue is presented and the conditioned responses they evoke. When one thinks of General Motors producing the Holden automobile in Australia through a local company, manned and managed by Australians, the idea that it is a citizen of America doing business in a foreign land becomes little more than a figure of speech that gets in the way of thoughtful analysis. An American company goes abroad to make money; almost never does it serve—consciously or otherwise—as an instrument of American national policy. Yet, since atavism plays a persistent part in the reactions of nations, people still confuse the present with an earlier century when such corporate entities as the East India Company were expected to force a British version of civilization on the *indigenes*.

Today our efforts to use the multinational company as a mechanism for extending United States laws and policies extraterritorially are aberrations, while instances where the CIA has employed American companies as cover have been blown up beyond life size. Though Japanese companies are probably more responsive to the wishes and strategies of their home government, the issue seems more emotional than real. Nonetheless, the fear, pervasive in poor countries, that such companies may become the entering wedge for economic imperialism is a political fact that cannot be ignored.

To remove political suspicion and resentment, it has long seemed to me necessary to denationalize the multinational company in exchange for some form of supranational citizenship created by multilateral treaty. My conception is quite modest. I am not suggesting a federal governmental structure at the world level, or anything like it. I have spent too much of my life on the exposed steppes of diplomacy and international politics to have any faith in such an ethereal design. What I propose—indeed, what I first proposed seven years ago in a speech in London—is something far more limited: that we seek to establish by treaty an international companies' law, administered by a body made up of representatives drawn from signatory countries, which would not only exercise normal domiciliary supervision but would also enforce the kinds of arrangements that are normally included in treaties of establishment. Each company that elected to apply for a charter under that law would agree to be bound by its provisions. Each state signing the treaty would accept guidelines limiting it in imposing restrictions on companies so chartered. The operative standard defining those restrictions would reflect the intention to assure the ability of host nations to defend their national interests with minimum encroachment on the interests of other states, while still preserving the freedom needed to protect the central principle of efficient resource use.

In order to qualify for a world charter, a company domiciled in a signatory state might have to meet certain conditions—such as, for example, that it operate in a certain minimum number of countries, that a minimum percentage of its shareholders reside outside the country of domicile, that its board of directors and its top command be multinational according to some fixed formula, and so on. From the point of view of the world community, the advantage of this approach is that the whole of the corporation's activities could be placed under international surveillance, so that such matters as transfer pricing and the adjustment of its accounts could not be artificially manipulated to the disadvantage of any signatory state. The inducement to the company to acquire a world charter would be the protection given it against destructive interference at the local level by a host country.

Obviously such an international company would have a central base of operations. It would not, like Muhammad's coffin, be suspended in the air, since it is clearly necessary that there be a single profit center. And its operations in its home country would, of course, be subject to local law to the extent that the organic treaty did not contain overriding regulations.

I recognize, of course, that a company will not become effectively a citizen of the world merely by a legal laying on of hands. It requires something more than an international companies law to validate its passport; the enterprise must in fact become international. This means among other things that share ownership in the parent must be widely dispersed so that the company cannot be regarded as the exclusive instrument of a particular nation which, in view of the underdeveloped state of most national capital markets, even in economically advanced countries, is not likely to occur very soon. But, over the long pull, as, in more and more countries, savings are effectively mobilized for investment, companies should assume an increasingly denationalized character, while we might, at the same time, expect a gradual internationalizing of boards of directors and parent company managements.

I offered these suggestions in tentative and speculative terms, recognizing that these were not the only means through which a solution might be sought. One could envisage an international treaty, for example, directed solely at resolving jurisdictional conflicts or limiting national restrictions on trade and investment. Yet an international companies act, as I saw it, would have intrinsic merits. It offered the best means I could think of to preserve for all society the great potential of the world corporation.

Nor was such a proposal, after all, far beyond the realm of present-day contemplation. It was merely an adaptation in a larger arena of what is likely to be created within the next few years in Europe: a common companies law for the European Economic Community together with a body of regulations to be administered by the European Economic Commission.

In suggesting the possibility of a multinational supervisory agency, I would avoid enmeshing it in the bloc-ridden machinery of the United Nations, or even, in the first instance, attempting to gain signatories outside the small circle of industrialized nations. Like the GATT, it would be regarded primarily as a mechanism for creating a code of rules among the major trading nations, but with the hope that, over the years, it might provide a world charter as more and more of the less developed countries adhered to its provisions.

Obviously, this is not a propitious season for spacious ideas but an interlude of flabby governments and squalid improvisations. Thus now is not the time for such a proposal to prosper; nor is anything serious likely to be done along this line for some years. Nevertheless, if we are concerned about creating and preserving an institutional means for using world resources efficiently, some mechanism in this general pattern will probably be necessary.

That brings us to a final question—the significance of the multinational company as an institutional form. Presumably because an article I once wrote was more elliptical than I intended, some critics seem to have drawn the curious inference that, with the development of multinational companies, I expected nation-states to wither away. To be sure, I did suggest—as I have today—that, in its present form, the nation-state is not adequate to meet the full requirements of modern business. I have even applied such disparaging adjectives as *archaic* and *obsolete*. But to suggest that an institution is archaic or obsolete is not to imply that it will "wither away." Most of the institutions by which men live are archaic and obsolete, since there is a frictional lag between the requirements of a changing world and man's ability to evolve his institutions to deal with them effectively. So, obsolete or not, the nation-state, as I see it, is here to stay—at least for a very long time—though I would hope that improvements can be made to adapt it more effectively to the rapidly changing world scene.

What role the multinational corporation may play as an evolutionary form, existing alongside the nation-state and perhaps helping to bridge the gap to the future, is hard to predict. In facilitating the mobility of resources, it serves, in my view, a useful purpose and, if nations do find the will and the way to shape cooperative arrangements for its supervision, these arrangements might themselves contribute to the ultimate design of a more spacious structure.

Beyond that, any prophecy seems presumptuous.

Index

The American Assembly
COLUMBIA UNIVERSITY

The American Assembly was established by Dwight D. Eisenhower at Columbia University in 1950. It holds nonpartisan meetings and publishes authoritative books to illuminate issues of United States policy.

An affiliate of Columbia, with offices in the Graduate School of Business, the Assembly is a national educational institution incorporated in the State of New York.

The Assembly seeks to provide information, stimulate discussion, and evoke independent conclusions in matters of vital public interest.

AMERICAN ASSEMBLY SESSIONS

At least two national programs are initiated each year. Authorities are retained to write background papers presenting essential data and defining the main issues in each subject.

About sixty men and women representing a broad range of experience, competence, and American leadership meet for several days to discuss the Assembly topic and consider alternatives for national policy.

All Assemblies follow the same procedure. The background papers are sent to participants in advance of the Assembly. The Assembly meets in small groups for four or five lengthy periods. All groups use the same agenda. At the close of these informal sessions, participants adopt in plenary session a final report of findings and recommendations.

Regional, state, and local Assemblies are held following the national session at Arden House. Assemblies have also been held in England, Switzerland, Malaysia, Canada, the Caribbean, South America, Central America, the Philippines, and Japan. Over one hundred institutions have co-sponsored one or more Assemblies.

ARDEN HOUSE

Home of The American Assembly and scene of the national sessions is Arden House, which was given to Columbia University in 1950 by W. Averell Harriman. E. Roland Harriman joined his brother in contributing toward adaptation of the property for conference purposes. The buildings and surrounding land, known as the Harriman Campus of Columbia University, are fifty miles north of New York City.

Arden House is a distinguished conference center. It is self-supporting and operates throughout the year for use by organizations with educational objectives.

AMERICAN ASSEMBLY BOOKS

The background papers for each Assembly program are published in cloth and paperbound editions for use by individuals, libraries, businesses, public agencies, nongovernmental organizations, educational institutions, discussion and service groups. In this way the deliberations of Assembly sessions are continued and extended.

The subjects of Assembly programs to date are:

1951——United States–Western Europe Relationships
1952——Inflation
1953——Economic Security for Americans
1954——The United States' Stake in the United Nations
——The Federal Government Service
1955——United States Agriculture
——The Forty-Eight States
1956——The Representation of the United States Abroad
——The United States and the Far East
1957——International Stability and Progress
——Atoms for Power
1958——The United States and Africa
——United States Monetary Policy
1959——Wages, Prices, Profits, and Productivity
——The United States and Latin America
1960——The Federal Government and Higher Education
——The Secretary of State
——Goals for Americans
1961——Arms Control: Issues for the Public
——Outer Space: Prospects for Man and Society
1962——Automation and Technological Change
——Cultural Affairs and Foreign Relations
1963——The Population Dilemma
——The United States and the Middle East